Dear Christian Parents

An Appeal for Homeschooling

Dear Christian Parents

An Appeal for Homeschooling

Stacey Durham

www.DearChristianParents.com

Dear Christian Parents: An Appeal for Homeschooling
by Stacey Durham

ISBN 978-0615519487

www.DearChristianParents.com

Printed in the United States of America

To Valerie,
The heart of our home

Contents

Preface

As I write these words, there are literally thousands of books readily available to anyone who wants to learn about homeschooling. Does there really need to be another one? Yes, I think so, and I'll tell you why.

The majority of the homeschooling books currently available are written for parents who have already decided to homeschool. Among these are books for use in teaching specific subjects, such as mathematics, history, the sciences, and language arts. There are also many books that teach the various homeschooling methods, such as the Charlotte Mason method, classical education, Montessori schooling, unschooling/child-led learning, and unit studies. There are even books that teach parents how to manage a homeschool in areas such as record keeping, grade reporting, and legal issues.

Such books are necessary and useful for homeschoolers, but they are of no use to parents who don't homeschool. These parents don't need how-to homeschool books, but they do need information to help them make the best choices for their children's education. Of course, they likely know about public schools and private schools already, but they probably don't know much about educating their own children at home. They need books that explain homeschooling to them.

For these parents, there are a number of books available that give good reasons for homeschooling, but the need is greater than the supply. All parents need to be made aware of homeschooling so that they will at least consider homeschooling as a serious, viable option for their children's education. Until this happens, books and other resources that promote homeschooling should be flooding the market. Those of us who advocate homeschooling need to do as much as we can to get the word out about this excellent form of education.

Of course, my special interest is in reaching Christian parents who are not homeschooling. I want them to see the connection between a child's education and his faithfulness to God throughout life. If this book can accomplish one thing, then I hope it is to prove to Christian parents that homeschooling is the most effective means of education by which they can pass their faith on to their children. If seeing their children carry on the Christian faith is the most important goal of parents, then this point alone will convince them to homeschool.

At present, it seems that this vital message about homeschooling has still not reached most Christian parents. Most of them are still sending their children to public schools and have never considered doing anything else. Many of them have heard the news that most children from professing Christian families are now growing up to turn away from the Lord, but apparently they don't see education as a major factor in this trend. I want to show them that education is indeed a major factor so that they will take charge of their children's education and help reverse this trend of apostasy.

My hope for this book is to reach those Christian parents who don't know about homeschooling and even those who don't want to know. (Parents who don't want to know about homeschooling are afraid they will be convinced and have to change. May their fears be realized!) I am seeking to capture their attention long enough to present sound reasons and arguments in favor of homeschooling. I want them to be aware of their opportunity to educate their own children and cause them to make a conscious decision regarding homeschooling. Even if they decide not to homeschool, I at least want them to have the chance to make that decision rather than remaining unaware of homeschooling.

To me, this book is not really a book. Instead, it is a series of letters bound together in book form. Each chapter is in fact a letter from me to Christian parents (hence the title) and a few other selected recipients. I wrote it this way not as a gimmick but as an effective means of communication. The art of letter writing has mostly been lost in our modern age, but it is still a great way to send a message. After all, it is the way God chose to communicate many of the words now preserved for us in the New Testament. It is also a very personal way to present the appeal I am making. My hope is that Christian parents will read these letters in the same way they would read any other personal correspondence from their friends or family. I truly want to connect to them as a brother in Christ.

I have grouped these letters into three different parts. The first part (chapters 1-6) contains my strongest Biblical arguments in favor of homeschooling. My hope is that most Christian parents who read these letters will be convinced to homeschool by the end of the sixth letter because of the strong Biblical evidence presented. These letters form the foundation of my appeal.

The second part (chapters 7-16) is intended to give Christian parents some information that is essential for understanding education in America today. Some of that information may be slightly tedious to read (history, citations of legal cases, etc.), but the content of these chapters is necessary for explaining the truth about public schools, parental rights in education, socialization, and other issues. The more Christian parents know about these issues and the Biblical principles involved, the better prepared they will be to make wise and godly decisions concerning their children's education.

The third part (chapters 17-25) presents some Scriptural guidance for those who have become convinced that homeschooling is the right choice for their children. Although these letters are not intended to be a how-to guide for Christian homeschooling, I do have some foundational, Biblical advice for Christian families who choose to homeschool. This includes specially targeted advice for fathers, mothers, and even children.

Note that I have included a glossary at the end of the book. Glossary terms within the chapters are shown in bold type. I selected these terms for the glossary either because they were uncommon or else they have particular importance in my message.

Thus, I offer my heart-felt appeal for homeschooling to all Christian parents. I hope and pray that God is rightly glorified in these pages, that His word is used accurately, and that you are edified in truth. Thank you for reading, and may God bless you.

Part I – My Biblical Appeal

1

Introductions, Purposes, and Goals

Dear Christian Parents,

"Grace to you and peace from God our Father and the Lord Jesus Christ." What better greeting could I offer to you than this one, which is used to introduce many of the letters in the Bible's New Testament? It seems appropriate for me to borrow these words as I salute you, my fellow Christians. Therefore, I say to you in all sincerity, may God bless you all with grace and peace through our Lord and Savior Jesus Christ.

In all likelihood, you and I have never met. Even so, I have so much to say to you. I realize that you are probably not in the habit of taking advice from strangers. Then again, maybe you are. Do you watch television, listen to the radio, read newspapers, or search on the internet? If you do, then you are already hearing and reading strangers' advice. So then, I hope you don't mind giving me a chance, for what I have to say is among the most important things that can be said to Christian parents.

So that we don't remain strangers, let me introduce myself to you. You really don't need to know very much about me, but a few things are essential. I am a Christian, just like you are. I am also a husband and a father, just as you are also spouses and parents. I believe that the Bible is the inspired word of God, and I'm sure you agree. I am also sure you agree that we Christians must use God's word as a guide for every part of life. As you can see, you and I have many things in common, and the most important of these is our shared faith in the Lord Jesus. It is on this basis that I appeal to you as a brother in Christ for a chance to make my case from the Bible to you.

Now let's talk about you. Even though we have probably never met before, I already know who you are. I have sought out you Christian parents because I know your goals and values. Because you are Christians, I know that you love the Lord. I also know that you love your children. Just knowing these two things about you is enough for me to know that what I have to say will be important for you.

You are concerned about your children's education as most parents are. Your children's studies, teachers, classmates, and schools are important to you. You are concerned about what they are learning both academically and socially. You probably worry that they will be exposed to so many bad things that you hear about in schools – violence, substance abuse, sexual promiscuity, etc. You want your children to have the best education, but you also want to protect your children from evil influences. Can you have it both ways?

If I told you that your children can have the best education from the best teachers in the best environment, would you believe me? What if there was a school that taught exactly what you wanted your children to learn? Would you send them there? What if this school had teachers and administrators whose sole agenda was the spiritual, physical, and mental wellbeing of your children? What if this school was perfectly safe from all threats to your children's minds, bodies, and, most importantly, souls? How much would you be willing to sacrifice to allow your children to attend this school?

Such a school is available to your children if you will only realize it. Regardless of where you live in the United States, your children can attend this school. In this school, you will have the power to oversee every moment of your children's education. You will choose your children's subjects, books, activities, and even their teachers and classmates. Moreover, when your children are in this school, you will know that they are perfectly safe.

This school is **homeschool**. We call it homeschool because it is usually taught within the home, but it is more accurate to say that it is within the family – parents and children included. This school goes wherever the family goes, and its classroom is anywhere they choose. All that is needed for your children to attend this school is for you to open its doors and get to work.

Because this school is within your home and your family, **the Lord is welcomed and honored in this school every day. Prayer and the Bible are also welcome there.** Because you Christian parents will be the teachers of this school, the lessons given will be completely focused upon educating your children in compliance with God's will. God's truth will be the foundation of everything your children learn in this school, and your children will be drawn closer to God every day. You will never have to "un-teach" any of the lessons that are taught to your children because everything they learn will be true to God's word. In this school, nothing will be introduced to your children without your permission. Your children will never be exposed to the filth and corruption of the world except to uncover the truth about sin and wickedness according to the word of God.

By now, you have begun to see the goodness of what I am imploring you to do. Truly, this is only the beginning, for I have much more to say on this matter. This is the first in a series of letters I have planned for you in which I will make my case from the Bible in favor of homeschooling. Please give me your patient, continuous, undivided attention, and I will do my best to make this case to you.

For now, I hope that you will carefully consider the appeal I am making to you. **Please, for the sake of your children, take on the vital task of educating your own children for yourself.**

I know that I am calling upon you to make a radical change and a tremendous commitment. However, let me remind you that when you devoted yourselves to Christ, you made a radical change and a tremendous commitment, and when God blessed you with children, you made another radical change and another tremendous commitment. Really, I am only asking you to carry out these changes and commitments to the full extent of God's will.

I also know that you have a lot of questions: Are you qualified to teach your children? Can you afford to homeschool? What about socialization? Is it harmful to shelter your children from the world? Will your children be prepared for college? How do you get started? I hope to answer these questions and much more in future letters.

Please understand that my purpose in these letters is not to present a comprehensive explanation of the academic benefits of homeschooling. Certainly, I could prove to you by facts, statistics, and test scores that homeschooled students typically outperform both public and private school students across the board in academics, but that is not my purpose. There are many other resources that make that case very well, and I encourage you to research those resources as you consider homeschooling.[1] If you check the academic record of homeschooled students, then you will be impressed, but I want to make a different impression on you.

My purpose in these letters is to reinforce a spiritual appeal to you on behalf of your children through the application of the Bible. **My goal is to convince you to educate your children in the best way to cultivate faithfulness to God within them.** Nothing else is as important as faith in God, for none of us can please God without it. Therefore, if a child's education fails to produce godly faith in him, then it is worthless, for it has failed to prepare him for the very purpose of his life.

As we go forward, I will ask you to prayerfully study both the Old and New Testaments with me as we seek the will of God regarding the education of our children. If you don't agree with my conclusions in these letters, then I respect your opinion and judgment with all honesty, sincerity, and truth. These letters are not intended to judge you or condemn you for any decision you make, but I do hope to influence you.

Until my next letter, please be thinking and praying about what I have introduced to you here. May God bless you and your family.

Regards in the Lord,
Stacey

---

[1] Many excellent resources are available in the "Homeschooling Research" section of the Home School Legal Defense Association website, nche.hslda.org/research.

2

Change Your Mind

Dear Christian Parents,

Did my first letter get you thinking? I hope so because there is a lot for you to think about. There is so much that God's word has to say on the subject of educating our children that we need to devote some serious thought to it. However, before we get deep into the Scriptures, I want to make sure we get off on the right foot.

Let me begin by defining a few terms for you. These may not be textbook definitions, but they are the meanings of words and terms I will use throughout these letters. Some of these terms overlap, but I will try to be as consistent with them as I can. When I use the term **school**, I am referring to any institution in which instruction is given to children and young people, whether it is administered by a government, a church, a private enterprise, or even a family. By **formal school**, I mean a school that is taught by professional teachers in a formal classroom environment. **Public school** is formal school that is open to the general population. **Compulsory school** is formal school in which attendance is compelled and forced by law. **Government school** is another term for compulsory school that emphasizes its government control and funding. **Private school** is a formal school for a limited clientele that is administered by a non-government entity and is an alternative to compulsory school. **Church school** is a type of private school that is administered by a local church or denomination. **Homeschool** is an *informal* school that is administered to children by their parents.

With all of those terms now defined, let's consider your thoughts about school. Of course, I can't read your mind, but chances are that you have never really thought much about sending your children to school. I don't mean that you haven't thought about your children's education, for I'm sure that you have. What I mean is that you probably haven't considered whether there is a better alternative than sending your children to a formal school where they will sit in classrooms, listen to professionally trained teachers, and receive instructions, homework, tests, and grades.

Most of us simply don't think about the alternative to formal school. This is because formal school is all that we have ever known. We have always been told that every child must go to school, period, end of story. That's the way it is, that's the way it has been, and that's the way it always will be. As a result, we have mindlessly conformed to the presumed mandate that when our children reach the appointed age (whatever that is), it is necessary to turn them over to the professionals for their education. We are truly compelled to send our children away for five days every week to be schooled.

The truth is that compulsory school has not always been the standard for children throughout history. It hasn't even been the standard throughout the history of the United States. From ancient times through early American history, it was generally understood that families were responsible for overseeing the education and training of their own children. This understanding is evident in the original 1828 edition of Noah Webster's dictionary, which defined **education** in part by stating, "To educate children well is one of the most important duties of parents and guardians" and "…an immense responsibility rests on parents and guardians who neglect these duties."[2]

Regrettably, governments later subverted that parental responsibility by asserting themselves as the most suitable sources for children's education. The idea of compulsory state education can be traced back to the Greek philosopher Plato (427-348 B.C.), who believed that children belong to the state and should be taught by government educators. Historically, there have been some governments that took the responsibility of educating children away from parents, but the colonial, state, and federal governments of

---

[2] Definitions of "educate" and "education" from Noah Webster, *American Dictionary of the English Language* (reprinted Chesapeake, VA: Foundation for American Christian Education, 1967).

America did not begin this way. Over time, the system of compulsory government schools became the standard of education in our country, and it has now been in place since the late nineteenth century. Because several generations of Americans have now been brought up in this system, it is difficult for the current generations to perceive of anything other than compulsory state-run schools or similar private alternatives. As a result, it never occurs to us to question the system. I am asking you to question it now. In future letters, I will give you more details about the history of compulsory schooling, but for now, just recognize that the modern, common practices of schooling have not always been the norm.

Thankfully, homeschooling is a legal alternative to compulsory schooling in the United States. Parental rights regarding homeschooling are sometimes challenged, and in some states homeschooling is heavily regulated, but homeschooling remains legal in all fifty states as I write this letter. (I'll have more to say about parental rights in the matter of education in a later letter.[3]) In the year 2010, more than two million students were homeschooled in the United States, and that number seems likely to increase in the coming years.[4] Hopefully, more and more parents will discover this alternative and seize this great opportunity for their children.

Unfortunately, the alternative of homeschooling is still not on the radar of most parents. By now, most parents have heard of homeschooling, but they usually don't consider it for a variety of reasons. Most often, homeschooling simply does not fit with their lifestyle. Both parents are usually so busy that they do not have time to educate their own children. Many parents are so deep in debt that their time is consumed by earning enough money just to keep current with their bills. Some parents are intimidated by the prospect of such a huge undertaking, and they don't feel qualified for the job. Others don't consider homeschooling because they have been given the wrong impression about it. They have accepted the stereotype of homeschooled students as maladjusted geeks or religious lunatics. They have not been exposed to the

---

[3] See Chapter 10, "Parents' Rights and the Return of Homeschooling."

[4] Brian D. Ray, "2.04 Million Homeschool Students in the United States in 2010," National Home Education Research Institute, 1/3/11. Retrieved 4/14/11, from www.nheri.org/HomeschoolPopulationReport2010.html.

goodness of homeschooling and its tradition of bright, productive, engaging, law-abiding, God-fearing graduates.

If you have any negative feelings about homeschooling, then I am hoping that my letters will change your mind about this excellent alternative to formal schools. I want you to become so convinced about homeschooling that you will be willing to make some serious sacrifices and changes for the sake of your children even if you have obstacles like debt. You can find a way to educate your own children at home if you are truly willing. It is even possible for you to homeschool with both parents working, but it won't be easy. Be assured that God can make it possible for your family to homeschool if it is His will, but you will first have to be fully convinced in your own mind that it is the right thing for you to do. My purpose right now is to give you that conviction.

As I told you in the last letter, the intent of my letters is to convince you through a Biblical viewpoint to teach your children yourselves rather than sending them to school. My goal is to persuade you to educate your children in the best way to cultivate faithfulness to God within them. Because you are Christians, I know that you trust the Bible as God's word, and so this may seem like an easy evaluation. However, you may be surprised how difficult it can be to let go of some of the worldly notions that have been covertly programmed into your mind. The idea of teaching your children at home may move you out of your comfort zone. You may even find yourself looking for reasons to refute the plain teachings of the Bible because those teachings contradict everything that you have been taught about children and education.

This is why I urge you now to change your thinking before you even open your Bible. **Make the decision now that you are going to be completely open-minded to the Scriptures.** Be prepared to set aside any notions that conflict with the truth of the Bible, no matter how ingrained or mainstream those notions may be. Apply the wisdom of Romans 12:2 to this evaluation that you are about to begin: "And do not be conformed to this world, but be transformed by the renewing of your mind, so that you may prove what the will of God is, that which is good and acceptable and perfect." Look at that again – **"prove what the will of God is."** What is God's will for the education of your children? How can you prove it, that is, how can you find out that it is true and good? The answers are in the word of God, and the proof is in the application of those answers. Let the Bible transform your mind regarding the education of your children, and don't conform to the ways of the world. Be ready even to change your mind about what a good (emphasize *good*) education really is.

Therefore, set your mind to seek the will of God regarding the education of your children and have confidence. God knows that your children need a good education, and you can trust that He will provide a way for them to have it if you will follow His direction. Regarding our most needed things, the Lord has taught us the right way to pursue them in Matthew 6:32-33:

> For the Gentiles eagerly seek all these things; for your heavenly Father knows that you need all these things. But seek first His kingdom and His righteousness, and all these things will be added to you.

While the "Gentiles" (unbelievers) around you seek to educate their children by the ways of the world, you will find a truly good education for your children when you seek the ways of God. In Matthew 7:7-11, our Lord promises:

> Ask, and it will be given to you; seek, and you will find; knock, and it will be opened to you. For everyone who asks receives, and he who seeks finds, and to him who knocks it will be opened. Or what man is there among you who, when his son asks for a loaf, will give him a stone? Or if he asks for a fish, he will not give him a snake, will he? If you then, being evil, know how to give good gifts to your children, how much more will your Father who is in heaven give what is good to those who ask Him!

Indeed, when you pursue the good and right way for your children's education, you are assured by your heavenly Father of success. There is no better guarantee in life than a promise from the Father.

As you now set your mind to pursue God's ways for the education for your children, let me give you one more message of encouragement: don't be afraid to be weird. Realize now that if you determine by the Scriptures that home-based education is the right thing for you to do, then you are not going to be in the majority. That doesn't matter. I know you, and you are the kind of people who will do what you think is right regardless of what others think. Follow the motto of Davy Crockett, who wrote, "I leave this rule for others when I'm dead, be always sure you're right—then go ahead!"[5] I will warn you that even some of your Christian friends will think you're strange. **Don't let them discourage you.** Better yet, give them this set of letters and change their minds!

In my next letter, I will begin to make a strong case from the Bible for why you need to teach your own children. Until then, keep an open mind and an open Bible, and keep discarding some of those old notions about school.

Regards in the Lord,
Stacey

---

[5] David Crockett, *A Narrative of the Life of David Crockett of the State of Tennessee* (Philadelphia: E. L. Carey and A. Hart, 1834), p. 1. Retrieved 7/13/11 from www.archive.org.

3

Nobody Else's Business

Dear Christian Parents,

Now that we have set the tone for how we are going to approach this evaluation of home-based education versus formal schooling, we are ready to dive in to the Bible. In the next few letters, I will make my strongest arguments from the Scriptures in favor of homeschooling. With open minds and open Bibles, let's get started.

It is always good to begin at the beginning, so let's go all the way back to the first family – Adam, Eve, and their children. Adam and Eve brought sin into the world when they ate the forbidden fruit (Genesis 2:15-17; 3:1-7), and they suffered the consequences of their actions. One of those consequences to the woman was the multiplication of her grief in childbirth (Genesis 3:16). So then, are we to believe that children are a punishment for sinful parents? Actually, it is quite the opposite.

Notice what Eve said when she gave birth to her first child: "I have gotten a man-child with the help of the LORD" (Genesis 4:1). Eve attributed the birth of her son to the power of God. She did not consider the child to be a punishment even though she suffered the tribulation of childbirth. Rather, she considered her child to be a gift from God, and she glorified God because of him. She exemplified the truth that Christ taught when He said, "Whenever a woman is in labor she has sorrow, because her hour has come; but when she gives birth to the child, she no longer remembers the anguish because of the joy that a child has been born into the world" (John 16:21). Eve expressed this same joy and glory to God again when she gave birth to Seth, for she said, "God has appointed me another offspring..." (Genesis 4:25).

Eve's words reflect a common principle found in Scripture concerning children. This principle is that children are a tremendous blessing of great value. Often in the Scriptures, the blessing of children is shown to be a measure of prosperity for both men and women (for examples, see Genesis 33:5; Deuteronomy 28:4, 11; Job 42:12-13; Psalms 113:9; 127:4-5; 128:1-6; Proverbs 17:6). There are many Bible examples of barren women who were overjoyed when God finally gave them the precious blessings of children, such as Sarah (Genesis 11:30; 21:1-2, 6-7), Rebekah (Genesis 25:21), Rachel (Genesis 29:31; 30:1-2, 22-24), Hannah (1 Samuel 1:2, 10-11, 20), and Elizabeth (Luke 1:7, 14, 36-37). These mothers demonstrated the truth of Psalm 113:9 – "He makes the barren woman abide in the house as a joyful mother of children. Praise the LORD!" Hannah was so joyful for her son that she spoke beautiful and eloquent words of prayer and praise for God (1 Samuel 2:1-10).

All parents should have this same godly understanding about the value of their children. I want to emphasize this understanding as the theme for this entire series of letters. This theme is stated beautifully in **Psalm 127:3-5**. This is the keynote passage for these letters, and one I would recommend that you commit to memory. Here it is:

> **Behold, children are a gift of the LORD; the fruit of the womb is a reward. Like arrows in the hand of a warrior, so are the children of one's youth. How blessed is the man whose quiver is full of them; they shall not be ashamed, when they speak with their enemies in the gate.**

Indeed, children are a joyous gift and a reward from God to parents. If you read the King James translation of this passage, then you will see the word "heritage" instead of gift. In the original language of the Psalms, this word literally means "inheritance." **Each one of your children is an inheritance from God to you.** This places your children in a category with some other tremendously valuable things that are also classified as inheritance from God – eternal life (Matthew 19:29), His promises (Hebrews 6:12), the blessings of heaven (1 Peter 1:4), the testimonies of God (Psalm 119:111), etc. That is how valuable your children are!

Of course, you don't need me to tell you that your children are valuable. You know this better than anyone because you love them more than anyone. However, I want you to consider what it means to treat them as a precious gift and a valuable inheritance. Each child must be viewed as a treasure of potential that God has entrusted to you. What will you do with this treasure? If you are not careful and deliberate about the way you raise your children, you could be like the prodigal son, who thoughtlessly wasted the inheritance from his father (Luke 15:13). Needless to say, this is no way for a faithful Christian to handle the heavenly Father's inheritance. Instead, Christians need to be good stewards of God's precious blessings.

How can you be a good steward over God's inheritance? Let's notice Psalm 127:3-5 again and think about the symbols of the arrows and the warrior. "Like arrows in the hand of a warrior, so are the children of one's youth. How blessed is the man whose quiver is full of them..." In this figure, you are the warrior, and in your hands are the arrows, your children (the more, the better!). You can aim them at any target you choose. You may choose targets of worldly value – love of wealth, prestige, fame, athletics, etc. – or you may choose spiritual targets for your children – love of God and man, faith, virtue, righteousness, etc. Obviously, a good steward of God's inheritance will choose targets that conform to God's will. **It is your responsibility to aim your children at the right targets.**

This is why it is so important for you to take charge of your children's education. If you surrender your children to be educated by others, then you will let others take charge of your inheritance and choose the targets for your children. You will turn over God's inheritance to strangers, and you will let others assume your responsibility. You will take the "arrows" out of your hands and place them into the hands of people who do not care for your children as much as you do and who probably do not share your spiritual values. It is likely that you will even allow your children to be aimed at some targets that contradict God's word and your faith in every way.

Homeschooling is the only alternative to formal schools that allows you to manage every aspect of God's inheritance to you as God intended. It also keeps your "arrows" in your hands where they belong. The truth is that God gave your children to you for you alone to raise. They are your stewardship, and education is part of that stewardship. **You must raise your children like it is nobody else's business because it is nobody else's business.** You cannot outsource any part of this job and expect to get the same results you would get by doing it yourself. Nobody can do the job of educating your children as well as you can. I know this is true because it is the design of God, and He knows best. I hope that you know this, too.

In fact, we need to pause right now to correct our thinking on the matter of our children's education. I have been describing homeschooling as an alternative to compulsory government schooling, but in truth compulsory government schooling is the alternative. As I said in my previous letter, it was understood from ancient times through early American history that families were responsible for overseeing the education and training of their own children. I'll go even farther now to say that **it has always been God's design for parents to take charge of their children's education, and that has not changed.** Because Christians are to have a Biblical worldview, we need to consider God's design as the norm and anything else as the alternative.

This is a bold claim that I have just made, so I need to offer you Scriptural proof of it. That will be the subject of my next letter. Of course, I have already offered the first proof of my claim from Psalm 127:3-5, but there is much more that we need to consider.

For now, I once again appeal to you to thoughtfully and prayerfully consider educating your children at home. You have the ability to impart to your children that which no one else can give them. They are your inheritance from God and your arrows to aim at targets you choose. Don't deprive them of the graceful wreath of their father's instruction or the beautiful ornaments of their mother's teaching (Proverbs 1:7-9).

Regards in the Lord,
Stacey

4

Looking for a Pattern

Dear Christian Parents,

Near the conclusion of my last letter, I made the bold claim that **it has always been God's design for parents to take charge of their children's education, and that has not changed.** I also promised to give Scriptural proof of my claim, so this will be my purpose for this rather long letter. By the end of the letter, I hope to demonstrate that the concept of homeschooling is indeed found and endorsed within God's word.

I'll begin by admitting that there is no explicit commandment of Scripture that says, "Thou shalt homeschool." If the only way to validate my case in favor of homeschooling were to cite an explicit commandment with those exact words, then I wouldn't be able to prove my claim. However, explicit commandments are not the only basis for establishing Scriptural authority for a practice. Authority is also established implicitly when the text of the Bible suggests that certain things ought to be done. Likewise, there are also positive examples in which particular practices are shown to be founded and sanctioned by the authority of God. If I can demonstrate that homeschooling is approved by God's word in any of these ways, then I can build a Scriptural case for homeschooling even without a commandment that says, "Thou shalt homeschool."

To build my case, I intend to show that there is a Biblical pattern for the education of children that Christians would be wise to follow. After we consider several passages of Scripture and notice the Biblical pattern, I will ask you to consider which model of teaching children better fits this pattern – is it formal school in which children are taught by professional teachers in a classroom environment, or is it homeschool in which children are taught by their parents in their homes and wherever they go?

Before we look into the Scriptures, we need to consider the use of the Old Testament as a source of authority for Christians. We should recognize that Christians are not bound to observe the Law of Moses as Israel was, for Christ has fulfilled that Law and ratified His own covenant and testament (Matthew 5:17-19; Galatians 3:23-25; Hebrews 8:1-13). However, this does not mean that the Old Testament and the Law of Moses have no use for Christians. In fact, without the Old Testament, the New Testament would have no foundation or context. The New Testament repeatedly draws upon Old Testament history and wisdom and often quotes Old Testament passages, so Christians must look to the Old Testament and the Law of Moses for guidance and insight regarding God's will on many matters. The New Testament comments on the value of the Old Testament when it says, "All Scripture is inspired by God and profitable for teaching, for reproof, for correction, for training in righteousness; so that the man of God may be adequate, equipped for every good work" (2 Timothy 3:16-17). The New Testament declares that the examples of the Old Testament are written for our learning (Romans 15:4; 1 Corinthians 10:1-11) and that "the Law is good, if one uses it lawfully" (1 Timothy 1:8). Therefore, let us seek the profitable, good, and lawful use of the whole Bible in the matter of our children's education.

Now we are ready to delve into the Scriptures in search of a Biblical pattern for our children's education. As far as I know, the best place in the Bible to find such a pattern is in the Old Testament book of Deuteronomy. This book is part of the Law of Moses that was given to ancient Israel, and it contains three main passages that present a pattern for education. The first reference to this pattern is found in Deuteronomy 4:9-10 when Moses instructed the older generation of Israel to pass on their knowledge and experiences with God to their descendants. He said:

> Only give heed to yourself and keep your soul diligently, so that you do not forget the things which your eyes have seen and they do not depart from your heart all the days of your life; but make them known to your sons and your grandsons. Remember the day you stood before the LORD your God at Horeb, when the LORD said to me, "Assemble the people to Me, that I may let

them hear My words so they may learn to fear Me all the days they live on the earth, and that they may teach their children."

Later, in Deuteronomy 6:4-9, Moses expounded upon these words with a more detailed plan for the education of Israel's children in the word of God. Notice this passage:

Hear, O Israel! The LORD is our God, the LORD is one! You shall love the LORD your God with all your heart and with all your soul and with all your might. These words, which I am commanding you today, shall be on your heart. You shall teach them diligently to your sons and shall talk of them when you sit in your house and when you walk by the way and when you lie down and when you rise up. You shall bind them as a sign on your hand and they shall be as frontals on your forehead. You shall write them on the doorposts of your house and on your gates.

This plan was repeated yet again in Deuteronomy 11:18-21, but Moses added a promise for Israel. He said:

You shall therefore impress these words of mine on your heart and on your soul; and you shall bind them as a sign on your hand, and they shall be as frontals on your forehead. You shall teach them to your sons, talking of them when you sit in your house and when you walk along the road and when you lie down and when you rise up. You shall write them on the doorposts of your house and on your gates, so that your days and the days of your sons may be multiplied on the land which the LORD swore to your fathers to give them, as long as the heavens remain above the earth.

Regarding this promise, notice that Moses had also given it in Deuteronomy 4:40 – "So you shall keep His statutes and His commandments which I am giving you today, that it may go well with you and with your children after you, and that you may live long on the land which the LORD your God is giving you for all time." God repeatedly gave such promises to all the generations of Israel in conjunction with their learning and obeying His commandments (see Deuteronomy 5:16, 29, 33; 12:28; 32:46-47).

Having read these passages from Deuteronomy, we can construct a simple summary of God's plan for educating Israel's children by identifying its basic elements in general terms:

- Who were to be the teachers? The children's parents
- What were they to teach? The words of God
- How were they to teach? With diligence, repetition, and constant exposure
- Where were they to teach? In their homes and wherever they went together
- When were they to teach? When they sat, when they walked, when they lay down, when they rose up, i.e., all the time
- Why were they to teach? So their children would learn to fear God and keep His commandments

These elements comprise a very simple and yet divinely wise plan for educating children. I know of no other text of the Bible that reveals God's mind in the matter of children's education in more detail or clarity.

These passages from Deuteronomy appear to be a good basis for understanding a Biblical pattern for children's education, but there are unresolved questions. Does this pattern apply to Christians, or was it intended only for Israel? Is there any other evidence of this pattern in the Bible? Is this pattern only for the teaching of moral and spiritual truths, or can we apply it for other types of education, including subjects like math and science?

To answer these questions, let's take each element of the pattern and search for further evidence about them. Regarding the teachers of children, the Bible consistently appoints parents to this role. There are too many relevant passages to list them all here, so let's notice just a few examples.

- Abraham is an outstanding example of a parent-teacher, for he was chosen by God specifically because he would be a leader and teacher of his children and household (Genesis 18:19). Abraham is an especially good example for Christians because we are his sons by common faith (Galatians 3:7, 9, 29), and we should imitate him.
- The whole book of Proverbs gives evidence of all parents' responsibilities in teaching, for most of the Proverbs are

given as instructions from parents to their children. Notice a passage from the introduction of this book of wisdom in Proverbs 1:8-9 – "Hear, my son, your father's instruction and do not forsake your mother's teaching; indeed, they are a graceful wreath to your head and ornaments about your neck." Thereafter, many of the wise sayings of this book are explicitly addressed from a father to his children (1:10, 15; 2:1; 3:1, 11; 4:1-4, 10, 20; 5:1, 20; 6:1, 3, 20; 7:1; etc.), and it would seem that the whole book ought to be taught in this way.

- In Psalm 78:1-8, fathers were given the responsibility for teaching the word of God to their own children from generation to generation. While this passage appears to use the term "fathers" in the sense of forefathers, nevertheless it is an important instruction for individual fathers as well.

- We can even find evidence of the Biblical pattern of education in the numbering of the Levites for the temple service in 1 Chronicles chapters 23-26, for the Levite fathers were assigned the duties of teaching their children how to carry out their roles.

- In the New Testament, we have the explicit commandment for Christian fathers in Ephesians 6:4 – "Fathers, do not provoke your children to anger, but bring them up in the discipline and instruction of the Lord." This commandment gives Christian fathers a similar commission as the one given to Abraham.

- Likewise, Christian mothers are designated in the New Testament for the training and upbringing of children (1 Timothy 5:10; Titus 2:4), and they should be inspired by the examples of Lois and Eunice (2 Timothy 1:5; 3:14-15) as well as the "chosen lady" of 2 John.

- We should also take note of our Lord Jesus, who as a child lived in submission to His parents (Luke 2:51) and evidently learned the trade of carpentry from Joseph (Matthew 13:55; Mark 6:3).

These examples of Scripture are sufficient to firmly establish that parents are to be the primary teachers of children. They all support the pattern revealed in Deuteronomy.

As for the content of children's education, the Bible assigns it-self – the word of God – as the centerpiece and basis of all instruction for all ages. The examples I just gave regarding parents demonstrate this point, and so do many other passages of Scripture, such as Deuteronomy 31:13, Psalm 119, Proverbs 22:6, and 2 Timothy 3:16-17. The word of God and its resultant fear (reverence) for God is to be the "beginning" or foundation of all knowledge, wisdom, and understanding (Psalm 111:10; Proverbs 1:7; 9:10). This means that every subject should be taught with a Biblical worldview. A **Biblical worldview** is an understanding of all things that is founded upon the Bible. In other words, the Bible is the window through which any subject of education should be viewed. This applies not only for spiritual matters, but also for all other subjects, such as history (notice Deuteronomy 6:20-25; Joshua 4:1-11, 20-24; Isaiah 46:9-11) and science (for example, the creation account of Genesis 1). Moreover, the Bible warns against learning from worldly sources that can captivate the mind and contradict the Lord (Colossians 2:8). I will have more to say about having a Biblical worldview in a later letter,[6] but for now let's just note that the Biblical pattern requires for God's word to be the foundation of all education just as we saw in Deuteronomy.

The educational methods of diligence, repetition, and constant exposure to God's word are also consistent in the Bible. For the purposes of teaching and learning, we can find diligence commended in 2 Timothy 2:15 and 2 Peter 1:15, repetition employed in Romans 15:15 and 2 Peter 1:12-13, and constant exposure exemplified in Psalm 119:97 and Acts 15:21. A survey of all the teachers of God's word throughout the Bible will demonstrate that they used these methods throughout the ages. Once again, the pattern from Deuteronomy is confirmed.

Regarding locations for teaching children, the Biblical pattern gives no limitations, but it does commend the home. In my next letter,[7] I will give you a thorough explanation of this part of the Biblical pattern for education.

Likewise, the Biblical pattern for education does not give restrictions for times of education. Any time is a good time for

---

[6] See Chapter 17, "A Plan For Homeschool."

[7] See Chapter 5, "No Place Like Home."

learning truth. This part of the pattern from Deuteronomy can be demonstrated by the examples of Jesus, who taught while He was sitting (Matthew 5:1), walking (Luke 24:15), lying down (John 13:23), and rising up (Mark 11:20). Certainly, the Lord was teaching all the time.

Concerning the reasons for children's education, there are many, but they can be correctly summarized as the fear of God and the keeping of His commandments. In fact, the goal of all learning is succinctly given from a father to a son in Ecclesiastes 12:12-13:

> But beyond this, my son, be warned: the writing of many books is endless, and excessive devotion to books is wearying to the body. The conclusion, when all has been heard, is: fear God and keep His commandments, because this applies to every person.

This is exactly the purpose given in Deuteronomy for the education of Israel's children, and thus this part of the Biblical pattern is extended to "every person." All people need to learn to fear God and keep His commandments, and the best time for them to learn this most valuable lesson of life is during childhood. "Remember also your Creator in the days of your youth..." (Ecclesiastes 12:1).

Taken altogether, these passages of Scripture give us a clear vision of the Biblical pattern for children's education. The pattern is supported by diverse and extensive evidence, for the words of Deuteronomy are confirmed by a host of other Bible passages. It is also clearly applicable for Christians, for the Bible is consistent in this pattern in both Testaments, inside and outside the Law of Moses, and across the various dispensations of time. This pattern is right for God's people yesterday, today, and always. We also see that it is appropriate to follow this pattern for all matters of education, for the Bible does not separate morals from academics, but rather it teaches that God's word is the beginning of all knowledge, understanding, and wisdom.

The passages we have read firmly establish a Biblical pattern for the education of children, but there are other passages of Scripture that may present alternative patterns. I don't want to overlook those passages, so let's consider them here:

- There are the examples of Moses in Egypt from Acts 7:22 and Daniel and his friends in Babylon from Daniel 1:5. These might be cited as examples of compulsory government education, but education under bondage in a strange land hardly qualifies as a positive commendation or an approved example.

- There is also the example of the apostle Paul, who was educated at the feet of Gamaliel (Acts 5:34; 22:3). Such an arrangement (student and teacher, disciple and rabbi – see Matthew 10:24; Luke 6:40) was common among the Jews by the first century, but that does not mean it is the best pattern for us to follow for educating children. Paul's education with Gamaliel was not an example of primary education for a child, but rather it was a formal rabbinical training for a young man. This does not constitute a different pattern from the one in Deuteronomy, but perhaps it is a complementary one with a different, more specific purpose. A good application for such an arrangement would be an apprenticeship or a mentorship, which historically were common ways of training young men for their vocations or professions.

- There is another pattern for education involving the priests and Levites who taught the Law of Moses to Israel (Leviticus 10:8-11; Nehemiah 8; Luke 2:46; Acts 15:21). For certain, these men were charged by God with the responsibility of teaching, but there is nothing in Scripture to indicate that the scope of their work included the primary education of children. Instead, they taught the Law of God to the assemblies of God's people (including adults and children) in the public places (temple, synagogues, etc.). This teaching role by the Levitical priests in ancient Israel was more akin to the teaching role of evangelists, pastors, and teachers in the church today (Ephesians 4:11-12). These men have a responsibility for teaching God's word, but there is no mandate for them to take charge of the education of children.

- The only verse in the Bible where the word "school" is used is Acts 19:9, so let us consider this example (see vv. 8-10 for context). After Paul had spent three months in Ephesus

preaching the kingdom of God to the Jews in the syn-
agogue, he and the disciples withdrew to the school of Tyrannus, where he reasoned daily for two years. During this
time, all Jews and Greeks in Asia heard the word of the
Lord. We do not know who or what was taught in this
school before Paul arrived, but we do know that it became a
home base for the spread of the gospel in Asia. There is
nothing in this example to imply that the primary education
of children was in any way involved in this school. It seems
more fitting to perhaps consider this as a pattern for training preachers, for it is likely that those who learned from
Paul in the school of Tyrannus were heavily involved in
spreading the word of God throughout Asia.

- Two other passages that may be acknowledged are John
  7:15 and Acts 4:13, where it is recorded that the Jewish authorities considered Jesus, Peter, and John to be "unedu-
  cated and untrained men." One may attempt to use these
  passages to equate a lack of formal schooling with a lack of
  education, but that would be a misapplication. This is not a
  backwards commendation of formal schools, but rather it is
  simply evidence of the tremendous power of God within
  the Lord and His apostles. The Jews were marveling that
  this carpenter could teach in the temple and that these simple fishermen could stand before the court and argue with
  their most imminent leaders and scholars (including Gamaliel – Acts 5:34-39).

Thus, we see that none of these passages alter the approved,
Biblical pattern of education that we have observed.

We have gone a long way around to get to this point, but this
investigation of Scripture is important to prove that there is a Biblical pattern for the education of children that Christians would be
wise to follow. Now that we know the pattern, we are ready to answer the question: which model of teaching children better fits this
pattern? Is it formal school in which children are taught by professional teachers in a classroom environment, or is it homeschool in
which children are taught by their parents in their homes and
wherever they go? Look at the pattern again:

- *Parents are to be the teachers.* Homeschooling fits the bill, but
  formal schooling does not.

- *The word of God should be the basis of all teaching.* God-centered homeschooling meets this standard, and so does God-centered formal schooling. However, most formal schools are not God-centered because they are government schools. In their case, the word of God is excluded from all teaching.
- *Teaching should be done with diligence, repetition, and constant exposure.* Most teaching is done in these ways, but if the subject being taught is not founded on the word of God, then the methods are of no consequence. If we therefore combine this point with the previous point, then God-centered homeschools pass and most formal schools fail.
- *Teaching should be done in the home and wherever the family goes together.* Homeschooling follows this pattern. Formal schooling does not.
- *Teaching should be ongoing at all times.* Homeschooling allows this to happen. Formal schooling cannot.
- *Teaching should have as its purpose the fear of God and the keeping of His commandments.* God-centered homeschooling has this purpose, and so does God-centered formal schooling. However, most formal schools are government schools in which God and His commandments are completely neglected. Christian homeschools make it their goal to fear God and obey His will in all things.

With this analysis of Scripture and homeschooling, I have all confidence to conclude that **God-centered homeschooling fits each point of the Biblical pattern for children's education.** This analysis does not preclude formal schools, but it doesn't commend them either. I have simply demonstrated the Biblical pattern for education, compared it to the models of homeschooling and formal schooling, and determined that homeschooling is a better match. I acknowledge that various forms of formal schools existed even among the first century Jews, but I am only interested in conforming to the pattern that God approved. Ultimately, you will have to decide which you believe is better for your children – just be sure that you have a strong Scriptural basis for your decision.

Before I close, I want to go back to a point I made in the last letter. I said that we need to think of God's design for education as the norm and anything else as the alternative. Our thinking on this matter is important because it affects the way we approach educating our children. A truly good education is one that conforms to the Biblical pattern and results in our children fearing God and keeping His commandments. The Bible says that "godliness is profitable for all things, since it holds promise for the present life and also for the life to come" (1 Timothy 4:8). Your children need a godly education to prepare them for life on earth and the life to come. Who will teach your children by the godly, Biblical pattern if not you? Do you think that the compulsory government schools, where the false application of "separation of church and state" rules, will give your children any sense of God's place in history, science, or any other subject? (I'll have much more to say about the separation of church and state in another letter.[8]) In generations past, our relatives were at least taught to read in school by using the Bible, but those days are long gone. Today, your children's only hope for a godly education is you.

In my next letter, I will talk about why your home is the best environment for your children's education. I have only begun to make my case to you, so I urge you to stick with me throughout these letters to the end.

Regards in the Lord,
Stacey

---

[8] See Chapter 9, "The Separation of Church and State."

5

No Place Like Home

Dear Christian Parents,

I'm glad you are still with me because I still have a lot to say. Take your time reading these letters, and let them digest awhile. These things deserve some study, some meditation, and some prayer.

In my last two letters, I stated my case from the Bible for why you are the best teacher of your own children. I have shown that your children are your inheritance and stewardship from God and that the Biblical pattern for education would have you to be your children's teachers. Now I will make my case for why your home (or wherever you are) is the best place to teach your children. This case is not hard to make, but some of those old notions about school might complicate things. Let's go ahead and toss those notions aside so they don't get in our way.

Before I talk about your home as a center for your children's education, I want to give a disclaimer concerning public schools. I will have much to say about public schools in these letters, and virtually none of it will be good. I do not mean to imply that there is nothing good about any public school, but rather I am looking at the public school system as a whole. All public schools have certain things in common because they are governed by the same laws, funded by the same governments, and designed and influenced by the same education professionals. I will be highly critical of this public school system, but I am not intending to offend anyone by the things I have to say nor am I assigning blame to anyone in particular. I'm not a snob about public schools, for I attended them for my entire academic career. I had some wonderful teachers in school who were genuinely good people, and I know that there are still many good teachers today. However, not even the good teachers can overcome something that is broken and fundamentally flawed. Christians who work in the public schools do the best they can to be good influences on the students they teach, but they are severely limited by the rules and laws that govern them. I simply want you to see the plain truth about the government school system. It just is what it is

With that disclaimer out of the way, I will begin to make my case in favor of your home by giving you a rather vivid and unflattering comparison: **public schools are like public restrooms.** I know that this may seem a bit crude, but it is the perfect comparison to make my point. I also realize that this is certainly not an argument from Scripture, but it is an argument from common sense. Common sense says that no one enjoys going into a public restroom – people only go when they have no other choice. Public schools are much the same way. Most parents send their children there because they think there is no other choice. However, there is another choice: keep the children at home.

Really, you could make the comparison of public schools to any public entity – public restrooms, public transportation, public swimming pools. Do any of these bring pleasant images to your mind? It seems that all of the filth and nastiness of the world condenses in public places, so why should schools be an exception? Think about it: wouldn't you much rather make use of your own restroom in your own home than use one in the corner gas station? Wouldn't you rather drive your own car than ride on a city bus? Wouldn't you rather swim in your own pool than swim at the city park swimming pool? Of course, you would always choose your own private alternatives when you could. Why should your children's education be any different? If your experience with all things public has been as disgusting as mine has, then how could you ever believe that public schools could be some utopia for educating children? Common sense tells you that your own home is a much better place for your children.

I'll have much more to say about problems in the public schools in later letters, but for now let's focus on the place that God has designated as the center for your children's education: your home. In my previous letter, I quoted from Deuteronomy 6:4-9 and noted that the people of Israel were instructed by God to teach their children in their homes and wherever they went. If it was good for Israel's children, then it should be good for our children, too. That standard of home-based, parent-guided education is still the best model for us to imitate today. It is the Biblical pattern that Christians would be wise to follow.

Consider for a moment what your home really is. It isn't only a place where your family goes to eat and sleep. Your home is an environment that helps you and your family members to become and remain the people that God wants you to be. God designed the home to be a place of love, where a husband loves his wife (Ephesians 5:25), a wife loves her husband (Titus 2:4), parents love their children (Proverbs 3:12; 13:24; Titus 2:4), children love (honor) their parents (Ephesians 6:2), and all love God (Matthew 22:37). God also meant the home to be a place of worship, where prayers, songs, Bible study, and meditations give all other functions of the home spiritual meaning and show that all is done in the service of God. Every God-centered home and every member of such a home should have as their mission statement, "As for me and my house, we shall serve the Lord" (Joshua 24:15b).

If your home is indeed what God intends for it to be, then there is no better place of learning and instruction for your children. We can take a lesson from the example of Cornelius, who "feared God with all his household" (Acts 10:1-2). This atmosphere of a God-fearing home was the perfect place for godly instruction, for Cornelius, his family, and his friends learned the word of God in his home, and they obeyed it (Acts 10:24, 44-48). Likewise, your God-fearing home is the very best place for your children to learn the word of God or any other instruction.

Of course, we have been led to believe that the hallowed halls of our nation's schools and universities are the best learning environments, but the word of God says otherwise. Notice **Proverbs 24:3-4 – "By wisdom a house is built, and by understanding it is established; and by knowledge the rooms are filled with all precious and pleasant riches."** The spiritual nature of the Scripture dictates that this passage is not simply describing the construction of a material building and its furnishings, but rather it speaks of the establishment and character of a God-centered home. Because a God-centered home is founded upon wisdom, understanding, and knowledge according to God's design, it is the best environment to learn these assets. In other words, the home is the best place to get an education, for what is an education if not the acquisition of wisdom, understanding, and knowledge?

Others may argue that public schools are built upon greater wisdom and understanding than the home, but do not be deceived. It may seem that a place employing many college-educated teachers and administrators must contain greater knowledge than a home-school with just two parents, but that impression is shown to be false when evaluated on a Biblical basis. Your God-centered home holds infinitely more knowledge than the public schools for one simple reason: "The fear of the LORD is the beginning of wisdom, and the knowledge of the Holy One is understanding" (Proverbs 9:10; see also Psalm 111:10; Proverbs 1:7). The fear and knowledge of God that exist in your Christian home make it a far better place to educate your children than even the best public schools, for the fear of God and the knowledge of His word were removed from public schools years ago. Those schools cannot even begin to give your child a proper education. Their teachers are trained to avoid God and the Bible altogether.

Maybe Dorothy from *The Wizard of Oz* said it best when she said, "There's no place like home." As simple as it sounds, it is a profound truth that there is no place like a God-centered home to teach, promote, and preserve the most important things in life. No government institution, no public school, and no social program can substitute for a strong, God-centered home life. Likewise, no private school and no church can provide your children with the loving instruction, spiritual strength, and godliness that you can provide them in your own home. I am not dismissing or condemning all formal schools by any means, but rather I am simply pointing out what is best in terms of godliness. Nothing can ever rival the home.

Not only is your home the best place for your children, but your children are good for your home. One reason that modern families suffer is because they are rarely ever together at home. I have never understood why so many parents seem to do all they can to keep their children away from home. They send their children away to school all day long, and then they enroll them in every extracurricular activity that they can possibly manage. They run from place to place with the idea that this is good for the children, and then they come home, eat, do homework, and crash in the bed. What kind of home life is that? How can God be the center of a home when no one is there? How can fathers bring up their children in the discipline and instruction of the Lord (Ephesians 6:4) and mothers be workers at home (Titus 2:5) when the family is always away from home doing other things? Proverbs 27:8 says, "Like a bird that wanders from her nest, so is a man who wanders from his home." Today, we have an entire culture of birds who have wandered from their nests. This is why homeschooling is good for the home: it puts the family together in the home where they belong.

When you and your children are together at home, all of you will benefit. The time you spend in educating your children at home will give them the advantage of your loving instruction and guidance, and it will make you better parents and better people. If you have ever taught others in any subject, whether it was a Bible class at church, a cooking lesson, a lesson on how to drive a car, or anything else, then you know how much you can gain by teaching. As your students are benefited by learning something new to them, you are benefited by becoming a master of a subject you already know. You may have to become a master of some subjects you don't know at all. Homeschooling will become a daily "renewing of your mind" (Romans 12:2) and a second chance at education for you. Because that education is Bible based, the result for you and your children will be transformational for your entire home.

There is one other issue that I must bring to your attention, and that is the issue of your children's physical, emotional, and spiritual safety. If you follow the local news, then you know that hardly a week goes by without a story of abuse by a teacher, an administrator, or a student in a local school. These stories should open your eyes, for when you turn your children over to others, you lose control over them. In a government school, you are not allowed to choose your children's teachers, classmates, or the lessons they are taught academically or socially. You are putting your children at risk of irreparable damage every time you leave them at school. Nobody whose child was in some way abused in a public school or a private school ever intended for that to happen. They were all surprised and horrified. Even so, they sent their children into that dangerous environment every day without a thought. Don't let it happen to your child.

If you choose to homeschool your children, then there is no possibility that your children will be entering one of those abusive situations because they will be staying in your home. You will have complete control to choose their teachers, classmates, and lessons. You will not allow someone to enter your home to abuse your children physically, emotionally, or spiritually. In your home, you are in control of what happens to your children. There is no safer place for them.

Are you convinced yet? Well, I'm not done – not by a long shot. I told you in my first letter that my goal is to convince you to educate your children in the best way to cultivate faithfulness to God within them. In my next letter, I will elaborate on that noble goal and tell you why it is the key to your greatest joy. I will present one of the most convincing points in favor of homeschooling, which is that homeschooled children are much more likely to stay with their parents' faith than children who attend public schools. Because you are Christians, I know that nothing could be more important to you than to see your children walking with the Lord. For now, I urge you to keep thinking and praying about the decision that I've asked you to make. May God bless you and your family.

Regards in the Lord,
Stacey

6

No Greater Joy

Dear Christian Parents,

For all that I have written to you so far, there is really only one goal, and that goal is for you to educate your children in the best way to cultivate faithfulness to God within them. There are many secondary goals for your children's education that are also important, but nothing matters more than their relationship with the Lord.

Therefore, it is imperative that you set your priorities accordingly. Make every effort to put your children in the best environment for them to succeed at what matters most, which is in faithfulness to God. At the same time, do not trouble your own family (Proverbs 11:29) or place stumbling blocks before your children that will hinder their faith. Jesus said, "Whoever causes one of these little ones who believe to stumble, it would be better for him if, with a heavy millstone hung around his neck, he had been cast into the sea" (Mark 9:42). How much more is this true for parents who cause their own children to stumble!

We can take a lesson on priorities for our children from the book of 3 John. The apostle John wrote this brief letter in his old age to a Christian by the name of Gaius. Gaius was not John's son in the flesh, but John counted him as a child in the faith. Consider the introduction of this letter in the first four verses:

The elder to the beloved Gaius, whom I love in truth. Beloved, I pray that in all respects you may prosper and be in good health, just as your soul prospers. For I was very glad when brethren came and testified to your truth, that is, how you are walking in truth. I have no greater joy than this, to hear of my children walking in the truth.

It is evident from this reading that Gaius' prosperity and health were important to John, but they were not his highest priorities. What mattered most to John was the spiritual prosperity that Gaius had already achieved, and he emphasized this by saying that it was his greatest joy to hear of his children walking in the truth.

The lesson about our children from John's letter to Gaius is this: **our children's spiritual wellbeing must have priority over everything else.** I am confident that most Christians are aware of the Bible's mandate to make spirituality a higher priority than physicality and materialism (consider Matthew 6:24-34), but that awareness has not always translated into action. All Christian parents desperately need to take this lesson to heart.

Most parents today wear themselves out supplying what they consider to be their children's physical, material, and social needs, but many neglect their first priority – their children's spiritual needs. They may give lip-service to spirituality, but everything they do exposes their true ambition for their children, which is worldly success. Instead of this, parents need to embrace the meaning of John's statement to his spiritual child Gaius – **"I have no greater joy than this, to hear of my children walking in the truth"** – and then do everything necessary to obtain their greatest joy. Parents must make their children's spiritual success their highest ambition and then work to achieve it by constantly and consistently teaching them the truth, showing them godly examples, and protecting them from ungodly influences. While other things may be important, they are distantly secondary to spiritual success in the Lord.

Children can become the source of Christian parents' greatest joy, but they can also be the source of their most painful sorrow and regret. For children to become the greatest joy of their parents, they must be brought up in the righteousness, wisdom, faith, and truth of Christ's word, i.e., the "discipline and instruction of the Lord" (Ephesians 6:4). If children are successfully raised in this godly way, then they will grow up to be men and women who walk in the truth, and their parents will realize their greatest joy.

On the other hand, while Christian parents may experience some satisfaction in their children's worldly success, there will be no lasting joy in a child who grows up, gets a good job, makes lots of money, has lots of friends, achieves worldly success, and is lost without the Lord Jesus Christ. For Christian parents who lose their children to the world, there will be only grief and bitterness. These truths are expressed in a few of the Proverbs that contrast the joy of parents whose children are wise versus the grief of those whose children are fools:

> A wise son makes a father glad, but a foolish son is a grief to his mother. (Proverbs 10:1)

> A wise son makes a father glad, but a foolish man despises his mother. (Proverbs 15:20)

> He who sires a fool does so to his sorrow, and the father of a fool has no joy. (Proverbs 17:21)

> A foolish son is a grief to his father and bitterness to her who bore him. (Proverbs 17:25)

> The father of the righteous will greatly rejoice, and he who sires a wise son will be glad in him. Let your father and your mother be glad, and let her rejoice who gave birth to you. (Proverbs 23:24-25)

Now let's go back to the goal of my letters to you: to convince you to educate your children in the best way to cultivate faithfulness to God in them and thus to achieve your greatest joy. I am convinced that homeschooling is the best way to achieve this goal and that public schooling is the worst. I have already given Scriptural, logical, and factual reasons for my opinion in previous letters, and I will give many more reasons in future letters, so I won't expound upon these reasons now. However, there are some important statistics that also support this point of view that I would like to share with you.

According to a survey conducted by Dr. Brian D. Ray of the National Home Education Research Institute, homeschooling is a highly effective way for Christian parents to impart their faith to their children. Dr. Ray's research involved more than 5,000 adults who had been homeschooled for at least seven years, so the sample size and subjects were more than adequate to validate the results. Of those surveyed, 94 percent agreed to the statement, "My religious beliefs are basically the same as those of my parents."[9] Many other topics were covered in this research, such as college, career, and community service, but this finding regarding homeschooled children's retention of their parents' faith is the single most significant result as far as I am concerned. To me, this proves that home-based education does indeed achieve the foremost goal of Christian parenting.

These findings do not mean that 94 percent of homeschooled children become faithful Christian adults. This simply means that 94 percent of homeschooled children retain the religious beliefs of their parents. If their parents were atheists, then there is a 94 percent chance that they became atheists. If their parents were Muslims, then there is a 94 percent chance that they became Muslims. In your case, because you are Christian parents, this statistic means **you have a 94 percent chance of passing your faith in Christ on to your children if you educate them at home.** If your goal is indeed to cultivate faithfulness to God in your children, then you have to love the odds of success through homeschooling.

So how do these findings compare for children who attend public schools? Several different resources have all discovered the same answer, which is that most public school students turn away from God. One resource is given by the Nehemiah Institute, which is an organization that provides Biblical worldview testing and training services. Over a period of twenty years, the Institute has conducted the PEERS (politics, economics, education, religion and social issues) test to evaluate worldview understanding in young people. More than twenty thousand students have been evaluated, and the results show that **85 percent of public school students from families professing Christianity do not hold a Biblical worldview.**[10] Another study conducted by Dr. Robert Simonds of the Center for Excellence in Education produced a similar result. He surveyed professing Christian parents whose children had at-

---

[9] Brian D. Ray, *Home Educated and Now Adults*, (Salem, OR: NHERI Publications, 2004), pp. 60, 63, 71, 83.

[10] "PEERS Trend Chart" by the Nehemiah Institute, Inc. Retrieved 4/14/11 from www.nehemiahinstitute.com and www.worldviewalliance.com.

tended public schools for twelve years, and he found that 88 percent of those children either reject belief in Christ or lack a Christian worldview by high school graduation.[11] These statistics are further evidence that the public schools do not achieve our main goal of promoting faith in Christ within our children. In fact, the public schools accomplish the opposite effect by destroying our children's faith.

These findings are not surprising at all, for they demonstrate the good and the bad of the Bible's messages regarding the raising of children. The good part is the simple and profound truth of **Proverbs 22:6 – "Train up a child in the way he should go, even when he is old he will not depart from it."** The more "training in righteousness" (2 Timothy 3:16) that you give to your children, the more likely it is that they will not depart from the way of righteousness when they are older. The bad part is what happens when Christian parents fail to heed the dire warning of **1 Corinthians 15:33 – "Do not be deceived: bad company corrupts good morals."** In other words, if you allow your children to be exposed to ungodly influences and educated without God in the public schools, then you greatly increase the risk that they will be seduced by the world away from the Lord.

Honestly, the only real surprise is how any children manage to emerge from the public schools with any shred of faith intact. Those who are responsible for public schools have completely removed God's word from public education, and they would remove God from all publicly educated children as well. I'm sad to say that for the most part, this agenda is succeeding. (I'll have much more to say about the descent of public schools in my next three letters.)

Before I close this letter, I want to share a story of success in faithfulness with you. It is the story of a boy whose father was an unbeliever, but his mother and grandmother were faithful Christians. Those dear ladies took it upon themselves to pass their faith on to this boy and taught him the word of God while he was still a child. Because of this godly training, this young man grew up to become a world famous evangelist. He went on missionary journeys to strange and difficult places in order to spread the gospel of Christ where it had never been. He suffered much along the way,

---

[11] Dr. Simonds' work provided by Citizens for Excellence in Education on 2/22/11.

but he was a diligent, faithful worker for Jesus Christ who won many souls for the Lord. Do you know who he was? Of course, he was Timothy, the young preacher who was the original recipient of two of the New Testament letters. Notice what Paul had to say about Timothy's upbringing:

> For I am mindful of the sincere faith within you, which first dwelt in your grandmother Lois and your mother Eunice, and I am sure that it is in you as well. (2 Timothy 1:5)

> You, however, continue in the things you have learned and become convinced of, knowing from whom you have learned them, and that from childhood you have known the sacred writings which are able to give you the wisdom that leads to salvation through faith which is in Christ Jesus. (2 Timothy 3:14-15)

If you truly want to succeed in passing your faith in Christ on to your children, then follow the example of Lois and Eunice by teaching your children yourself. If you do, then you will very likely achieve your greatest joy.

I know that there are many other concerns that you have about your children's education, but let your mind be at ease. If you can achieve this one goal of passing your Christian faith on to your children, then I am convinced that all of the other secondary goals will fall into place. In fact, the Lord said as much when He said, "But seek first His kingdom and His righteousness, and all these things will be added to you" (Matthew 6:33).

I am hopeful that the evidence in this letter is enough to convince you to homeschool your children. If passing your Christian faith on to your children is most important to you, then the 94 percent chance of success in homeschool versus the roughly 85 percent chance of failure in public school should be enough for you to make your decision. However, if you still need more convincing, then I have more to share with you. There is so much more that we need to talk about concerning government schools, so please keep reading. May God continue to bless you and your family.

Regards in the Lord,
Stacey

POST SCRIPT

The statistics I cited from the Nehemiah Institute and the Center for Excellence in Education are results from surveys that were answered by persons who professed to practice Christianity. The respondents in these studies likely included persons from a variety of backgrounds, beliefs, and denominations. Obviously, I cannot account for the exact beliefs or religious activities of every person surveyed, so I offer these statistics to you as the best available information regarding the subject.

I have read reports of similar studies done by others (Josh McDowell, Dr. James Dobson) who found similar results, including one study conducted by a specific denomination, the Southern Baptist Convention (SBC). In that study, the SBC Council on Family Life reported that "88 percent of the children raised in evangelical homes leave church at the age of 18, never to return."[12] This SBC study is relevant because 85 percent of children from SBC families attend public schools. Perhaps you will interpret this as a reflection on the SBC and other evangelical churches and families rather than the public schools, but these results are consistent with the other studies. The truth revealed by these studies is that children who attend public schools are not likely to share their parents' faith.

---

[12] Jon Walker, "Family Life Council says it's time to bring family back to life," *Baptist Press*, 6/12/02. Retrieved 5/2/11 from www.bpnews.net.

Part II – My Appeal Expanded

7

The Original Intent
For Education in America

Dear Christian Parents,

In the next four letters, I will shift gears in order to provide some perspective for you about American education from a historical and legal viewpoint. The purpose of these four letters is to give you a sense of how the modern state of public schools came into being and how homeschooling returned from near extinction. I intend to show you how public schools have descended from their noble original intents to their current state of godlessness as the various levels of government became increasingly involved and God and the Bible were steadily squeezed out of the schools.

This history is important because it will show you that **the public schools of today cannot cultivate faithfulness to God in your children.** I want you to know about these things because it will provide further motivation for you to educate your own children at home. The fourth letter[13] will provide a message of encouragement for you by showing how the homeschool movement has emerged as a beacon of hope for godly families against the tide of godlessness.

I hope that you will be able to see the providential hand of God in the events and court decisions that I will describe to you. It may not seem at all providential when we consider how our public schools have degraded into complete secular **humanism**, but re-

---

[13] See Chapter 10, "Parents' Rights and the Return of Homeschooling."

member that God has often allowed those who resist Him to choose their own paths and suffer the consequences (Romans 1:24, 26, 28; 2 Thessalonians 2:10-12). At the same time, it is undeniably providential when we see the same courts that have eliminated any acknowledgement of God from the public schools' curriculum and activities have also recognized the rights of parents to educate their own children. I pray that Christian parents will now take hold of these rights and follow the lead of **providence** away from public schools and into the safety of their godly homes.

The sorry state of public schools may be the catalyst that God is using to convince parents to take their children out of a fundamentally bad and unbiblical system. As strange as it may seem, it may be that God allowed Himself and His word to be removed from these schools so that His people would remove their children also. In the midst of the disaster that is the public school system, our Lord seems to be saying to Christian parents and their children, "For I know the plans that I have for you, plans for welfare and not for calamity to give you a future and a hope" (Jeremiah 29:11). God is speaking to us Christian parents – let's listen to Him!

To begin our brief study of the history of American public education, let us consider the old colony of Massachusetts. Many times, Massachusetts has been "ground zero" for legislation and leadership in the matters of education and schools in the history of America. This history in Massachusetts began when the Pilgrims settled at Plymouth in 1620 and the Puritans with the Massachusetts Company settled at Salem and Boston by 1630. The Pilgrims and Puritans came to the New World to find religious freedom, so it is no surprise that their mode of education was religious. The first colonial school was started in Boston in 1635 (the Boston Latin School, a.k.a. the Roxbury Latin School), and the first college was chartered there in 1636 ("New College," later called "Harvard College" after a clergyman named John Harvard). The purpose of Harvard College was to train ministers of the gospel (typical of all early American colleges), and its original mottoes were *In Christi Gloriam* (For the Glory of Christ) and *Christo et Ecclesiæ* (Christ and the Church).

In 1642, the Massachusetts Bay Colony enacted the first law pertaining to education ever passed on the North American continent. You will be interested to know that it was essentially a homeschooling law, though of course it did not use that terminology.

This law required that certain men would be selected in each town to keep watch over the education of children and apprentices. They would verify that children and apprentices were being taught to speak and read English and that they knew the laws. They would also verify that the head of each household was instructing his household in religious principles at least once a week. Furthermore, it was required that a useful trade be taught in the home. Parents, guardians, and apprentice-masters who failed in these requirements would be fined and possibly suffer the loss of their children.[14]

In 1647, the first American law pertaining to public schools was also passed in Massachusetts. This was called "The Old Deluder Satan Act" because the first paragraph in the law recognized Satan's work in illiteracy as a means to keep man from understanding the Scriptures. As a defense against Satan's schemes, the law required any township with at least fifty households to hire a teacher to instruct children in reading and writing. Furthermore, any township with at least one-hundred households was required to set up a grammar school in order to prepare able young men for university attendance.[15]

Notice that these laws reflect the cold realities of the world from which these early colonists had come. They knew the cursed history of Europe's centuries in darkness when the people were immersed in illiteracy and ignorance of the Bible as the religious and political leaders ran roughshod over them. They knew very well the atrocities that came from those conditions, and they did not want to allow such sins to follow them into the New World. Europe was still in the gloom of such spiritual oppression, and only the late work of some of the Reformers (John Wycliffe, Martin Luther, John Calvin, William Tyndale, etc.) had given a glimmer of light for the common people to read the Scriptures for themselves. Now the colonists had a chance to start fresh and free of Europe's darkness, and they knew education was necessary for their spiritual and political success.

---

[14] Text of the Massachusetts Bay School Law (1642). Retrieved 4/14/11 from the Constitution Society website, www.constitution.org/primarysources/schoollaw1642.html.

[15] Text of The Old Deluder Act (1647). Retrieved 4/14/11 from the Constitution Society website, www.constitution.org/primarysources/deluder.html.

Practices and laws pertaining to education spread unevenly across the colonies. Most of the New England colonies adopted policies similar to Massachusetts regarding public schools. None of the colonies had government-sponsored, free public schools as we know them now. Some towns had small tax subsidies for schools, but families who sent their children to school paid tuition. Schools were generally operated by churches, and privately operated tuition schools were common. "Dame schools" were private schools in which a woman (dame) was hired by several families to educate their children, often in her own home. In the southern colonies, there were no formal public schools at all other than certain charity schools for the poor. Wealthy planter-class families hired tutors, employed private schools, or even sent their sons to European boarding schools. In most areas, parents educated their own children at home simply because it was the natural and Biblical approach. Many children were either too rurally located to have local schools or too busy helping in the family business to attend schools even if they were available. Most children's education was a combination of in-home instruction, church attendance, and work experience (chores, apprenticeships, etc.).

Throughout the early years of education and public schools in America, religion always had a prominent place. Regardless of how education was administered, practically all primary education in early America was of a Christian nature. There were never any publicly funded, compulsory, secular schools in the colonies as we have today. This was always true during colonial times and continued to be the case when the new nation of the United States was established.

The first U.S. law pertaining to education can be found in the Northwest Ordinance of 1789 (the same year the Constitution was ratified), which was a document that set the terms by which territories could become states. The Northwest Ordinance bound education and religion to government in its third article, stating, "Religion, morality and knowledge, being necessary to good government and the happiness of mankind, schools and the means of education shall forever be encouraged."[16] Consequently, states that entered

---

[16] Northwest Ordinance retrieved 4/14/11 from the Library of Congress website, www.loc.gov.

the union under the Northwest Ordinance included very similar language in their own constitutions. They codified in their laws that **schools and education should promote religion, morality, and knowledge.**

Let me pause to remind you that I am writing these particular things to you not to give you a tedious, step-by-step history of American education or to advocate for government-run public schools, but rather I seek to give you a benchmark to measure the original intent for education in America. To give you a better sense of this intent, I want to invoke the concept of **patriotism** in its literal sense. The word "patriotism" comes from the Greek word *patrios*, which means "of one's fathers." True patriotism is not simply loyalty to one's country, but rather it is loyalty to one's fathers.

So then, what did the founding fathers of our nation intend for education? Many of them were educated by their families in their homes (homeschooled) in their early years and spent very little time in formal schools, so their concepts of education were largely family oriented. Moreover, their concepts of education were founded on the Christian religion, and they intended for Christianity to remain an integral part of education. Consider some of their own words:

> You do well to wish to learn our arts and ways of life, and above all, the religion of Jesus Christ. These will make you a greater and happier people than you are. Congress will do everything they can to assist you in this wise intention. – GEORGE WASHINGTON, First President of the United States, speaking to Delaware Indian chiefs who sought to educate their children in American schools[17]

> Religion is the only solid basis of good morals; therefore education should teach the precepts of religion, and the duties of man

---

[17] George Washington's "Address to Delaware Indian Chiefs," on May 12, 1779; John C. Fitzpatrick, ed., *The Writings of George Washington from the Original Manuscript Sources: 1749-1799*, 39 vols. (Washington, D.C.: U.S. Government Printing Office, 1931-1944), Vol. XV, p. 55. Retrieved 4/14/11 from the University of Virginia website, etext.virginia.edu.

toward God. – GOUVERNEUR MORRIS, penman and signer of the Constitution[18]

It has been the error of the schools to teach astronomy, and all the other sciences, and subjects of natural philosophy, as accomplishments only; whereas they should be taught theologically, or with reference to the Being who is the author of them: for all the principles of science are of divine origin. Man cannot make, or invent, or contrive principles: he can only discover them; and he ought to look through the discovery to the Author. – THOMAS PAINE, author of *Common Sense*, who is generally considered to be the most unbelieving and irreligious of the founders because of his later writings in *The Age of Reason*[19]

Let divines and philosophers, statesmen and patriots, unite their endeavors to renovate the age by impressing the minds of men with the importance of educating their little boys and girls, inculcating in the minds of youth the fear and love of the Deity... and leading them in the study and practice of the exalted virtues of the Christian system. – SAMUEL ADAMS, The Father of the American Revolution[20]

You have, by the favor of Providence and the attention of friends, received a public education, the purpose whereof hath been to qualify you the better to serve your Creator and your country. – WILLIAM SAMUEL JOHNSON, signer of the

---

[18] Gouverneur Morris' "Notes on the Form of a Constitution for France," circa. 1792; Jared Sparks, ed., *The Life of Gouverneur Morris* (Boston: Gray and Bowen, 1832),Vol. III, p. 483. Retrieved 7/13/11 from books.google.com.

[19] Thomas Paine, "A Discourse delivered by Thomas Paine, at the Society of the Theophilanthropists at Paris, 1798", *Miscellaneous Letters and Essays, on Various Subjects, 1798* (London: W.T. Sherwin, 1817), p. 66. Retrieved 7/13/11 from books.google.com.

[20] From a letter to John Adams, October 4, 1790; Charles Francis Adams, *The Works of John Adams, Second President of the United States*, Vol. VI (Boston: Charles C. Little and James Brown, 1851) p. 414. Retrieved 7/13/11 from books.google.com.

Constitution, framer of the Bill of Rights, and first president of Columbia (King's) College[21]

In 1749, when Benjamin Franklin wrote "Proposals Relating to the Education of Youth in Pennsylvania," he advocated for religion in education and extolled "the excellency of the Christian religion above all others ancient or modern."[22] Franklin was not always an outstanding example of pious Christianity, but he certainly saw the necessity of educating children in the faith, both for his state and later for his nation.

The next quote is from Fisher Ames, who was a Representative in the First United States Congress and the primary author of the First Amendment. On August 20, 1789, he suggested the following wording for the First Amendment, which was adopted by the House of Representatives and altered slightly in its final form: "Congress shall make no law establishing religion, or to prevent the free exercise thereof, or to infringe the rights of conscience."[23] Did he intend for this clause to eliminate the Bible from American schools? Certainly not – consider his words:

[Why] should not the Bible regain the place it once held as a school book? Its morals are pure; its examples, captivating and noble. The reverence for the Sacred Book, that is thus early impressed, lasts long; and, probably, if not impressed in infancy, never takes firm hold of the mind. In no Book is there so good English, so pure and so elegant, and by teaching all the same they will speak alike, and the Bible will justly remain the standard of language as well as of faith.[24]

---

[21] From a speech to the first graduating class of Columbia College; Edwards Beardsley, *The Life and Times of William Samuel Johnson,* (Boston: Houghton, Mifflin and Company, 1886), pp. 141-142. Retrieved 7/13/11 from books.google.com.

[22] Benjamin Franklin, "Proposals Relating to the Education of Youth in Pensilvania" (1749), p. 22. Retrieved 4/14/11 from the University of Pennsylvania Libraries website, sceti.library.upenn.edu.

[23] *The Constitution of the United States of America: Analyis and Interpretation*, The Congressional Research Service, Library of Congress. Retrieved 4/14/11 from www.findlaw.com.

[24] Fisher Ames, *Works of Fisher Ames* (Boston: T.B. Wait& Co., 1809), pp. 134-135. Retrieved 7/13/11 from books.google.com.

The following quotes are all from Noah Webster, who was a Revolutionary War soldier, a legislator, a judge, a founder of Amherst College, an expert on languages, and the author of the dictionary that bears his name. Notice his understanding of education and religion:

> I should rejoice to see a system adopted that should lay a foundation for a permanent fund for public schools, and to have more pains taken to discipline our youth in early life in sound maxims of moral, political, and religious duties.[25]

> In my view, the Christian religion is the most important and one of the first things in which all children, under a free government ought to be instructed....No truth is more evident to my mind than that the Christian religion must be the basis of any government intended to secure the rights and privileges of a free people.[26]

> The Education of youth [is] an employment of more consequence than making laws and preaching the gospel, because it lays the foundation on which both law and gospel rest for success...[27]

> [S]elect passages of [the Bible]...may be read in schools, to great advantage. In some countries the common people are not permitted to read the Bible at all. In ours, it is as common as a newspaper and in schools is read with nearly the same degree of respect. Both these practices appear to be extremes. My wish is not to see the Bible excluded from schools, but to see it used as a system of religion and morality.[28]

---

[25] Rosalie J. Slater, "Noah Webster, Founding Father of American Scholarship and Education," preface from *American Dictionary of the English Language*, (reprinted Chesapeake, VA: Foundation for American Christian Education, 1967), p. 22.

[26] Ibid.

[27] Ibid. p. 12

[28] Noah Webster, "On the Education of Youth in America," *A Collection of Essays and Fugitive Writings on Moral, Historical, Political, and Literary Subjects* (Boston: I. Thomas & E.T. Andrews, 1790), p. 9. Retrieved 7/12/11 from books.google.com.

Dr. Benjamin Rush, signer of the Declaration of Independence and member of the Continental Congress, wrote an essay entitled "A Defence of the Use of the Bible in Schools" (1791). Can there be any doubt as to his attitude regarding Christianity in American education? Consider a few of his words:

> [T]he only foundation for a useful education in a republic is to be laid in Religion. Without this, there can be no virtue, and without virtue there can be no liberty, and liberty is the object and life of all republican governments.[29]

> I do not mean to exclude books of history, poetry, or even fables from our schools. They may and should be read frequently by our young people, but if the Bible is made to give way to them altogether, I foresee that it will be read in a short time only in churches and in a few years will probably be found only in the offices of magistrates and in courts of justice.[30]

> I lament that we waste so much time and money in punishing crimes and take so little pains to prevent them...we neglect the only means of establishing and perpetuating our republican forms of government; that is, the universal education of our youth in the principles of Christianity by means of the Bible; for this Divine Book, above all others, constitutes the soul of republicanism.[31]

> By withholding the knowledge of this doctrine [the Bible] from children, we deprive ourselves of the best means of awakening moral sensibility in their minds.[32]

---

[29] Benjamin Rush, "Thoughts Upon the Mode of Education Proper in a Republic," 1786; from James W. Fraser, *The School in the United States: A Documentary History* (New York: McGraw-Hill, 2001), p. 28.

[30] Ibid., p. 29.

[31] Benjamin Rush, "A Defence of the Use of the Bible in Schools" (American Tract Society, circa. 1830). Retrieved 4/14/11 from www.biblebelievers.com.

[32] Ibid.

Let the children who are sent to those schools be taught to read and write and above all, let both sexes be carefully instructed in the principles and obligations of the Christian religion. This is the most essential part of education.[33]

These are only a small sampling of the many quotes from our founding fathers that express their intentions for American schools, whether public or private, to teach religion, morality, and knowledge. They are unequivocal proof of our patriotic heritage concerning education.

From the brief history and the words of our nation's founders that I have given you, you can see the prominent place of religion in the beginning of the American educational system. If the public school system still had such noble goals as religion (specifically the Christian religion as intended by the early Americans), morality, and knowledge, then we would have little concern with the results today. However, the modern system is a far cry from that original intent.

So what has caused the public schools to progress from a mostly good beginning to the calamity we see today? What has happened to remove even the least vestiges of morality and religion from the public schools? I'll give you those answers in the next two letters. Until then, keep praying, reading your Bibles, and seeking for the best blessings of God upon your children.

Regards in the Lord,
Stacey

POST SCRIPT

I have presented the words of the nation's founders with some hesitation because some of them promoted government-run public schools over parent-led education or private schools, which obviously defies the purpose of my letters. Dr. Benjamin Rush and Noah Webster in particular believed that the states should adminis-

---

[33] Benjamin Rush, "To the citizens of Philadelphia: A Plan for Free Schools", March 28, 1787; Lyman H. Butterfield, ed., *Letters of Benjamin Rush*, (Princeton, NJ: American Philosophical; Society, 1951), pp. 412-415. Retrieved 7/13/11 from the San Diego State University, College of Education website, edweb.sdsu.edu.

ter education. Keep in mind that these men believed that the Bible should be taught in schools, so in essence they saw compulsory schools as a way of ensuring that all children were taught the Bible. Their motivations were honorable, but their proposed methods were not compliant with the Biblical pattern of education. They were likely influenced by the teachings of Martin Luther and John Calvin, who advocated for compulsory schools to take children away from parents and give them to the approved authorities for their education.

From a Biblical standpoint, I strongly disagree with anyone who favors compulsory government education. As you have read in my letters, I believe the Bible instructs parents, not the state, to be the educators of their children. The reason I have quoted these men in this letter is only because I want to demonstrate the truth about early American education and Christianity, namely that the founders always intended for the Christian religion to be not only a part of public schools but also the basis of education in America. On this point, I wholly agree with the founders' intent, but let us keep in mind that they were fallible, just as we all are, and their words and ideas are not in the same category as the word of God.

8

Common Schools, Evolution, and Humanism

Dear Christian Parents,

In my last letter, I gave you some of the early history for America's public schools in order to show you the original intent of our nation's founders regarding education. This letter will continue that summary of history and will show you how the public schools began to evolve into the calamity we see today. After reading this letter and the next one, you will see that **the public schools of today cannot cultivate faithfulness to God in your children.** In fact, these schools can only present obstacles to your children's faith. If your children's spiritual well-being matters to you, then you need to know about these things. When you know about these things, I believe you will want to educate your children at home.

Now to continue the story of public education, we again look to Massachusetts. There we find Horace Mann (1796-1859), who is known by many as "Father of American Public Education" or "Father of the Common School Movement." As the first Secretary of the first Board of Education of Massachusetts (the first board of education in the U.S.), Mann completely recreated the schools of that state. Mann became an advocate for the Prussian (German) system of education after visiting Prussia and seeing how well that system taught students to conform to unifying state mandates. He convinced the state government of Massachusetts to adopt the Prussian system, and it was enforced on the public by passing the nation's first compulsory school law in 1852.

Mann's Prussian system of education created the first true government schools in the nation. At first, the state simply funded existing public and private schools and required all children to attend them, but soon the state took control of their administration. Under Mann's system, all schools were linked together by districting into an educational structure unlike anything before. It compelled all children to receive the same, universal education via schools funded by taxpayers (hence the name **"common schools"**). It trained children to operate as cogs in the new industrial economy rather than individuals in the old agricultural/artisan economy. It taught children how to climb the social ladder by economic progress and system-approved character traits. It trained children to become good citizens of the republic and to obey orders. It did these things by employing certified teachers who were strictly and professionally trained in the system. Concerning these state-sponsored compulsory schools, the teachers employed by them, and their captive students, Mann arrogantly wrote, "We, then, who are engaged in the sacred cause of education, are entitled to look upon all parents as having given hostages to our cause..."[34]

One of the most detrimental effects of Mann's system was that it eliminated much of the substance of Christianity from the schools. Mann was a Unitarian, which means that he did not believe in the Trinity. In other words, Mann believed in God, but he did not believe in the eternal deity of Jesus Christ and the Holy Spirit (contrary to John 1:1 and many other passages of Scripture). He was supported by some wealthy Unitarians who helped to fund the first state teachers' college for Mann's new system. That system removed any teachings perceived to be divisive or sectarian (denominational) from its curriculum because the state needed uniformity among its citizens. While leaving a skeleton of general Christian morals (Ten Commandments, the golden rule, etc.), it eliminated some core doctrines, such as the triune nature of God, and shifted the emphasis to secularism.

Shortly after Massachusetts adopted Mann's system, other states began to follow. Little by little, the Mann system of compulsory, state-funded, district-organized public schools spread to all states,

---

[34] Horace Mann, *Lectures on Education* (Boston: Ide & Button, 1855), p. 184. Retrieved 7/13/11 from books.google.com.

with Mississippi being the last state to pass mandatory school laws in 1918. Can you still see Mann's influence on the public schools today? The one-size-fits-all approach, the slave-to-the-bell mentality, the pressure to fit in to the state-approved expectations, the group-first mindset, the pyramid structure – these are all staples of Mann's system that took the emphasis away from the original intent of public education. While the founders of the nation had seen that religion, morality, and knowledge were necessary for good government, Mann saw that other traits were necessary to make good workers – Prussian style.

Horace Mann may not be the worst villain in this story of public schools, but his work paved the way for greater villains that followed him. Unitarian beliefs and the emerging pressure of a new, industrial economy motivated Mann, but others who were motivated by pure godlessness built upon the groundwork Mann had laid. One of Mann's main liabilities in this story is that he took away the local, community-run aspect of individual schools and replaced them with a large, state-run conglomerate structure. Under Mann's system, public schools truly became government schools. This meant that public schools gained the force of government that would later be used to compel a godless education for all students.

However, even after Mann's reforms, public schools continued to read and teach from the Bible. Mann favored the use of the Bible in schools provided that it was taught without anything he considered to be sectarian. The public schools also continued to use the *New England Primer* (published from 1690-1900) and the *McGuffey Readers* (published from 1841-1960) as texts for instruction. These books were filled with Biblical references and moral lessons based on the Christian religion. Moreover, students even attended to prayers while in public schools. Mann's system emphasized the importance of a secular education and an intricate-control structure, but it did not eliminate religion and morality in the classroom.

In order for the Christian religion and its morality to be completely pushed out of the public schools, much more sinister influences would arise. Perhaps the greatest and most sinister of the influences on American public schools can be found in the person of Charles Darwin. In 1859, this Englishman published *On the Origin of Species by Means of Natural Selection, or the Preservation of Favoured Races in the Struggle for Life,* and his influence has grown immeasurably in the more than 150 years since. Darwin's book advanced the theory of evolution, which declared that all life had evolved from lower forms of life by the natural process of mutations over eons of time. Clearly, this theory conflicts with the Bible's account of creation, which declares that God made all things by His word in only six days (Genesis 1-2; Exodus 20:11). Not only this, but Darwin's theory also conflicts with actual science and has been debunked many times. Even so, the scientific community has accepted and built upon Darwin's theory, and today it is defended as a sacred creed and taught as an undeniable fact.

I cannot overemphasize the effect that Darwin's theory has had on public schools. It has now emerged to dominate the public schools in nearly every subject. In science, students are taught that everything exists as the result of random, fortunate accidents rather than the result of a loving Creator's purposeful design. In geography, students are taught that the features of the earth are the results of billions of years of natural processes because this timeframe is necessary for Darwinian evolution to have occurred. In history, students are taught an evolutionary view of societies that corresponds to man's evolution of wisdom and technology (**Social Darwinism**). In literature, students are made to read countless stories and books that have evolutionary theory built in as truth while the Bible is dismissed as a book of allegories and fables. I could go on and on, but it is enough to demonstrate that the theory of evolution and its resultant philosophy of humanism now rule in the public schools.

Speaking of humanism, you need to understand how humanism crept into the public schools and invited evolution along. Those who sought justification for disbelieving God and the Bible found a friend in Charles Darwin. The theory of evolution gave them an alternative to the Bible's account of creation, so they could now reject God in the name of so-called science. From this combination of factors, humanism was born (or at least it found new life).

Humanism is a philosophy that embraces human reason and experience as the only guides for human life. Because humanists believe that man is the most highly-evolved animal, they consider man to be in essence his own god who makes his own rules and destiny. The "promised land" of humanists is a utopian society that evolves from man's achievements in science and technology. This philosophy is a branch of humanism called **"positivism"** in which science is essentially substituted for God and the only truth is that which can be verified by science.

Late in the nineteenth century, the humanistic philosophy of thinking began making its way into American society and public schools. Without overtly declaring the tenets of Darwinian evolution or banning the teachings of God from the classroom, humanist teachers progressively began to shift the emphasis of education onto collective mankind and society. With the structure that had been established by Horace Mann and the compulsion of government, these humanist influences were able to spread rapidly through the whole system to every school and student.

One prominent humanist that you need to know about is John Dewey (1859-1952). He is known as the "Father of Modern Education" because of the tremendous influence he had over schools in America. Dewey was an atheist who did not believe in absolute truth but thought that all truth had to be experienced through experimentation. He claimed that nothing is inherently good or evil but that the value of anything is relative to its situation. The following words, which are attributed to Dewey, correctly summarize his views that are expressed throughout his voluminous writings.

> Faith in the prayer-hearing God is an unproved and outmoded faith. There is no God and there is no soul. Hence, there are no needs for the props of traditional religion. With dogma and creed excluded, the immutable truth is also dead and buried. There is no room for fixed, natural law or moral absolutes.[35]

Dewey was an evolutionist and a signer of the first Humanist Manifesto of 1933, which was a bold declaration of the atheistic creed of humanism. This manifesto rightly described humanism as a religion, and Dewey worked to spread that religion throughout the nation. His philosophy of education held that schools were not for the purpose of imparting knowledge or wisdom, but rather they were for social transformation. To Dewey, schools were a means of taking control of man's own evolution and preparing children for an ever-evolving society (again, Social Darwinism).

---

[35]Attributed to John Dewey, "Soul-Searching," *Teacher Magazine*, September 1933, p. 33.

By no means did Dewey accept the teaching of absolute religious or moral truths in schools. In his mind, the state (government) replaced God as the ultimate authority (the concept of **statism**). The beliefs of Dewey formed the philosophy that he spread to innumerable teachers and educational professionals through his lectures, books, and pamphlets for many, many years. Dewey's communistic, humanistic, and atheistic philosophy resounded when he wrote:

> I believe that every teacher should realize the dignity of his calling; that he is a social servant set apart for the maintenance of proper social order and the securing of the right social growth. I believe that in this way the teacher always is the prophet of the true God and the usherer in of the true kingdom of God.[36]

According to his book *Democracy and Education*, John Dewey intended to cause a societal transformation, and this is exactly what he did. To achieve his goal, Dewey did not attempt to start a sudden revolution, but rather he preferred the slow, evolutionary approach of progressivism. **Progressivism** produces gradual changes usually through governmental intervention. It is the real opposite of conservatism, for rather than conserving what already exists, progressivism seeks to change it. Dewey knew that a radical revolution for the cause of humanism would never succeed in America, but he thought a gradual progression (shall we say, evolution?) of humanism in public schools would slowly erode the country's tradition of Christian beliefs and constitutional heritage of personal liberty. By his progressive approach in the education of children, Dewey succeeded in transforming society almost without anyone noticing.

By 1930, humanism was already so prevalent in the schools that Charles Francis Potter, signer of the first Humanist Manifesto, wrote the following in his book *Humanism: A New Religion*:

---

[36] John Dewey, *My Pedagogic Creed* (New York: E.L. Kellogg & Co., 1897), p. 18. Retrieved 7/13/11 from books.google.com.

Education is thus a most powerful ally of Humanism, and every American public school is a school of Humanism. What can the theistic Sunday-schools, meeting for an hour once a week, and teaching only a fraction of the children, do to stem the tide of a five-day program of humanistic teaching?[37]

Indeed, little could be done, for the sheer imbalance of time made it nearly impossible to counteract the volume of godless teaching poured out on public school students. Keep in mind that this was the 1930's, and we have fallen a long way since then.

It didn't take very long for Dewey's societal transformation to start taking effect, and it has continued virtually unabated until today. Unfortunately, there is likely worse still to come. Consider the words of John J. Dunphy, another humanist, who described his vision of humanism's progress in 1983:

I am convinced that the battle for humankind's future must be waged and won in the public school classroom by teachers who correctly perceive their role as the proselytizers of a new faith: A religion of humanity that recognizes and respects the spark of what theologians call divinity in every human being. These teachers must embody the same selfless dedication as the most rabid fundamentalist preachers, for they will be ministers of another sort, utilizing a classroom instead of a pulpit to convey humanist values in whatever subject they teach, regardless of the education level: preschool, day care, or large state university.

The classroom must and will become an arena of conflict between the old and the new – the rotting corpse of Christianity, together with its adjacent evils and misery, and the new faith of humanism, resplendent in its promise of a world in which the never-realized Christ ideal of "love thy neighbor" will finally be achieved.[38]

---

[37] Charles Francis Potter, *Humanism: A New Religion* (New York: Simon and Schuster, 1930), p. 128. Cited by David Limbaugh, *Persecution: How Liberals Are Waging War Against Christianity* (New York: HarperCollins Publishers, 2004), p. 65. Retrieved 7/13/11 from books.google.com.

[38] John J. Dunphy, "A Religion For A New Age," *The Humanist,* (January-February, 1983) p. 26. Cited by Dr. D. James Kennedy, *Led by the Carpenter: Finding God's Purpose for Your*

Dewey and his fellow humanists did tremendous damage to the schools and culture of twentieth century America, but they didn't do it alone. Even with the takeover by Darwinian and humanistic forces in the public schools, greater forces were needed to satisfy the opponents of God. To completely force God and the Bible out of the public classrooms would require the full intercession of the government, and this would be accomplished through the judges and justices of our nation's court system. In my next letter, I will give you a summary of the court rulings that have finished the job that Dewey started.

Regards in the Lord,
Stacey

Life! (Nashville: Thomas Nelson Publishers, 1999). Retrieved 7/13/11 from books.google.com.

9

The Separation of
Church and State

Dear Christian Parents,

After reading my last two letters, you should have a good understanding of the descent of public education from the founding of the United States until the middle of the twentieth century. You have seen how public schools were steadily moved away from God and the Bible and toward Darwinian evolution and humanism. In this letter, I want to notice a few relevant court cases to provide you with an overview of the decisions that have been most responsible for removing God and the Bible from America's public classrooms. Case by case, the judicial system has eliminated "religion, morality, and knowledge" (ref. the Northwest Ordinance of 1789) as the purposes for schools and replaced them with secular humanism. You will see that the foundation of these decisions is a poor interpretation and application of a phrase that is not even found in the U.S. Constitution.

The first case of note is *Everson v. Board of Education*, which came before the U.S. Supreme Court in 1947. There were at least two significant precedents set in this case for American public schools. For one, the Court decided that the religious clauses of the First Amendment of the Constitution ("Congress shall make no law respecting an establishment of religion, or prohibiting the free exercise thereof") would govern not only the U.S. Congress but also all areas of government, which included state governments and even local boards of education. The Court did this by incorporating the First Amendment's religious clauses into the Fourteenth Amendment, which was a post-Civil-War amendment that was intended to prevent states from denying the civil rights of former slaves by requiring due process and equal protection for all citizens.

Notice that the Court focused on the word "establishment" in these religious clauses but ignored the word "Congress" (hence the term "Establishment Clause" rather than "Congressional Establishment Clause"). In effect, the Court decided that an act of a board of education on a local level is equivalent to an act of the U.S. Congress on the federal level when it concerns religion. If a local board of education permits the acknowledgement of Christianity in a public school, then it is as if Congress has passed a law to establish Christianity as the official state religion.

The other precedent from *Everson* was the use of a particular metaphor to interpret the religious clauses of the First Amendment. That metaphor was "a wall of separation between church and state." The Court lifted this phrase from a short letter written by President Thomas Jefferson in 1802 to a Baptist Association in Danbury, Connecticut. President Jefferson was responding to the Baptists' request for assurance that the wording of the First Amendment would not allow the federal government to interfere with the practice of religion. Jefferson guaranteed them that the First Amendment absolutely prevented the federal government from infringing on religion, "thus building a wall of separation between Church and State."[39] The Court took this phrase and made a giant leap by connecting it to the Constitution, interpreting it as the separation of religion and government, and creating a mandate for the complete secularization of public schools.

Notice the irony in this: Jefferson assured the Danbury Baptists that the First Amendment would keep the government out of religion, but now it is taught that Jefferson's intention was to keep religion out of the government with the effect being that government now tells religion what to do! Of course, Jefferson's letter was private correspondence that never should have been used by the Court as a key to interpret the Constitution (Jefferson had virtually nothing to do with writing the Constitution), but the Court didn't even use Jefferson's words accurately. Jefferson was alluding to a Refor-

---

[39] Thomas Jefferson's letter to the Danbury Baptists, January 1, 1802. Retrieved 4/14/11 from the Library of Congress website, www.loc.gov.

mation era concept which denied the "divine right of kings" (or governments) to manage churches, but the Court ignored the context of Jefferson's letter. In 1985, Supreme Court Chief Justice William Rehnquist lamented the Court's use of "separation of church and state," saying, "Unfortunately the Establishment Clause has been expressly freighted with Jefferson's misleading metaphor for nearly 40 years."[40] With the *Everson* case in 1947, the Court effectively changed the meaning of Jefferson's words, the meaning of the First Amendment, the meaning of the Fourteenth Amendment, and the course of the public school system. It would not be long until the Christian religion would no longer be welcome in American public schools.

The next year after *Everson v. Board of Education* – 1948 – the U.S. Supreme Court restated its conviction to the interpretation of "a wall of separation between church and state" in *McCollum v. Board of Education*. The plaintiff in this case, Vashti McCollum, was an atheist who later served two terms as president of the American Humanist Association (AHA). In their ruling, the Court decided that voluntary, parent-permitted religious activities in public schools are unconstitutional. In its opinion, the Court referred to the *Everson* case and declared, "The First Amendment has erected a wall between Church and State which must be kept high and impregnable."[41] The Court decided that the Constitution forbade a state from the "commingling of sectarian with secular instruction in the public schools."[42] Humanism won the day.

The next major brick in the wall of separation was set in 1962 when the U.S. Supreme Court ruled in the case of *Engel v. Vitale*. In its ruling, the Court decided that a short, nonsectarian prayer given in New York schools was unconstitutional. The prayer simply stated, "Almighty God, we acknowledge our dependence upon Thee, and we beg Thy blessings upon us, our parents, our teachers, and our Country."[43] In the explanation of the Court's ruling, Justice

---

[40] James Huston, "A Wall of Separation," Library of Congress Information Bulletin, Vol. 57, No. 6 (June, 1998). Retrieved 7/14/11 from Library of Congress website, www.loc.gov/loc/lcib/9806/danbury.html.

[41] *Mccollum v. Board of Education* , 333 U.S. 203 (1948).

[42] Ibid.

[43] *Engel v. Vitale*, 370 U.S. 421 (1962).

William Douglas, who concurred with the majority decision, undauntedly admitted that public schools had been altered from their original design when he wrote:

> Religion was once deemed to be a function of the public school system. The Northwest Ordinance, which antedated the First Amendment, provided in Article III that "Religion, morality, and knowledge being necessary to good government and the happiness of mankind, schools and the means of education shall forever be encouraged."[44]

Although implied by the Court, the First Amendment did not alter the educational mandate of the Northwest Ordinance, but rather it was the infiltration of humanism in the twentieth century that had done so. The broader application of the Court's ruling affected all public schools, for the Court agreed with the plaintiffs that "prayer in [the] public school system breaches the constitutional wall of separation between Church and State."[45] With this, prayer was no longer welcome in public school, and over the years it would be eliminated from graduations, sporting events, and extracurricular functions. A later decision by the Court (*Wallace v. Jaffree*, 1985) would even prevent moments of silence from being observed in schools for fear that the purpose of the silence might be prayer.

Another major brick in this wall was set the next year – 1963 – when the U.S. Supreme Court ruled in *Abington School District v. Schempp*. At issue was a Pennsylvania policy of opening the school day with a voluntary reading from one chapter of the Bible. The Court found this policy to be in violation of the First Amendment. The decision was influenced by "expert" testimony regarding the potential effect upon Jewish students, which the Court summarized by saying:

> But if portions of the New Testament were read without explanation, they could be, and ...had been, psychologically harmful

---

[44] Ibid.

[45] Ibid.

to the child and had caused a divisive force within the social media of the school.[46]

The effect of this ruling was that the Bible was no longer to be read in public schools. The Court did allow limited teaching about the Bible "as part of a secular program of education,"[47] but the Bible's morals and meaning are forbidden. Although religious and moral teachings from the Bible had been present in American schools since their inception and the First Amendment had been in effect for 174 years, the Court decided in this case that the whole system of education had always been in error and conflict.

In 1971, the U.S. Supreme Court established a new standard for evaluating legislation pertaining to religion in its decision in *Lemon v. Kurtzman*. This new standard, now known as the "Lemon Test," contains three tests according to the Court:

> Every analysis in this area must begin with consideration of the cumulative criteria developed by the Court over many years. Three such tests may be gleaned from our cases. First, the statute must have a secular legislative purpose; second, its principal or primary effect must be one that neither advances nor inhibits religion...finally, the statute must not foster "an excessive government entanglement with religion."[48]

The Court's decision struck down a Pennsylvania law allowing nonpublic school teachers to be reimbursed for teaching secular material. The broader effect is that all levels of government were further prevented from promoting the original purposes of education – religion, morality, and knowledge – for these purposes would never pass the Court's newly established secular tests.

In 1980, the U.S. Supreme Court's decision in *Stone v. Graham* prohibited the posting of the Ten Commandments in Kentucky public schools. A Kentucky statute had allowed posters of the Ten Commandments to be purchased with private funds and posted in classrooms, but the Court ruled the statute unconstitutional, saying

---

[46] *Abington School District. v. Schempp*, 374 U.S. 203 (1963).

[47] Ibid.

[48] *Lemon v. Kurtzman*, 403 U.S. 602 (1971).

it "has no secular legislative purpose"[49] (i.e., it violated the "Lemon Test"). In the Court's explanation of its opinion, it stated:

> If the posted copies of the Ten Commandments are to have any effect at all, it will be to induce the schoolchildren to read, meditate upon, perhaps to venerate and obey, the Commandments. However desirable this might be as a matter of private devotion, it is not a permissible state objective under the Establishment Clause.[50]

Notice that again: it is not a permissible state objective to teach children to obey such principles as are described in the Ten Commandments, such as obedience to parents and prohibitions against theft, murder, adultery, and lying. After almost 200 years, the last sparks of the founders' original intentions of religion, morality, and knowledge were finally being extinguished.

In 1987, the case of *Edwards v. Aguillard* resulted in the U.S. Supreme Court striking down a Louisiana law that required the Bible account of creation to be taught whenever evolution was taught in public schools. The Court explained its decision, saying, "…because the primary purpose of the Creationism Act is to endorse a particular religious doctrine, the Act furthers religion in violation of the Establishment Clause."[51] It did not completely forbid the teaching of creation, but it barely conceded that such teaching "might be validly done with the clear secular intent of enhancing the effectiveness of science instruction."[52] This is not much of a concession, for it is highly unlikely than any modern court will ever acknowledge that creationism can be taught with any secular intent. This decision further reinforced the humanists' long-standing goal of secularizing public schools.

Although not a court case, I should mention here the U.S. Department of Education's policy for "Religious Expression in Public Schools." This policy was adopted in August of 1995 by Secretary of Education Richard Riley at the request of President Bill Clinton

---

[49] *Stone v. Graham*, 449 U.S. 39 (1980).

[50] Ibid.

[51] *Edwards v. Aguillard*, 482 U.S. 578 (1987).

[52] Ibid.

and has been in force ever since. The policy allows public school administrators the discretion to honor parents' requests to have their children removed from classes involving religiously objectionable material, but it does not require them to do so. The policy states that **"students generally do not have a Federal right to be excused from lessons that may be inconsistent with their religious beliefs or practices."**[53] When parents' and students' rights in public schools become a matter of administrators' discretion, they are no longer rights but privileges to be granted or denied.

From the year 2000, notice the case of *Fields v. Palmdale*, which rendered an appalling judgment in the matter of sex education. In this case, some parents of public school children in Palmdale, California, "brought an action in district court against the School District and two of its officials for violating their right to privacy and their right 'to control the upbringing of their children by introducing them to matters of and relating to sex.'"[54] When the district court dismissed the case, it was appealed to the United States 9th Circuit Court of Appeals. The federal judges in that court then stated (emphasis added):

> We agree, and hold that **there is no fundamental right of parents** to be the exclusive provider of information regarding sexual matters to their children, either independent of their right to direct the upbringing and education of their children or encompassed by it. We also hold that **parents have no due process or privacy right to override the determinations of public schools** as to the information to which their children will be exposed while enrolled as students.[55]

In other words, when parents turn their children over to the state for education, they surrender all rights in regards to anything their children may be taught. By this judicial legislation, public school officials may teach students absolutely anything, and parents

---

[53] From "Religious Expression in Public Schools" by U.S. Secretary of Education Richard Riley, 1995. Retrieved 4/14/11 from the U.S. Department of Education website, www2.ed.gov/Speeches/08-1995/religion.html.

[54] *Fields v. Palmdale School District PSD*, No. 03-56499 (9th Cir. 2000).

[55] Ibid.

have no rights in the matter other than taking their children out of the public schools.

There are many other cases I could cite, but let's consider just one more from 2007. In the case of *Parker v. Hurley*, two sets of parents sued the school district of Lexington, Massachusetts, because their children were exposed to material involving homosexuality without their consent. A federal district court sided with the school district against the parents, and this decision was upheld by the United States 1st Circuit Court of Appeals in 2008. The U.S. Supreme Court refused to review the case, so the district court's ruling now stands as the law of the land. Of particular interest are the words of the district judge, Mark L. Wolf, who stated:

> Parents do have a fundamental right to raise their children. They are not required to abandon that responsibility to the state. The Parkers and Wirthlins may send their children to a private school that does not seek to foster understandings of homosexuality or same-sex marriage that conflict with their religious beliefs. They may also educate their children at home.[56]

Notice that the judge recognized three options for parents in the matter of education: send their children to private school, educate their children at home, or **abandon their parental rights and responsibility to the state in the public schools**.

Indeed, you have a fundamental right to raise your children, but when you turn them over to public schools for their education, you completely surrender that right and allow them to be exposed to anything the administration chooses to present, including sex education, homosexuality, evolution, and any other ungodly influence. Moreover, you submit your whole family to the intrusion of public school administration, for even your children's time at home will be dominated by homework. Your family's schedule will be dictated by the public school schedule, and if you do not comply, then you will be in violation of truancy laws. Lately, many schools even seek to control the food children may eat and the clothes they may wear. Your children's healthcare also will become subject to school control, for they cannot attend public schools without certain vaccina-

---

[56] *Parker v. Hurley*, 474 F. Supp. 2d 261 (D. Mass. 2007) and No. 07-1528 (1st Cir. 2008).

tions and tests. Likewise, if your child becomes sick and misses school for a few days, then you will be will be required to provide a physician's excuse or else be in danger of legal penalties. Furthermore, if school officials determine that your child needs mind-altering drugs to control his behavior (Ritalin, Adderall, etc.), then they can pressure you and even threaten you to comply. If that isn't bad enough, some schools consider the provision of contraceptives and transportation to abortion clinics as part of their healthcare responsibilities. That judge wasn't kidding about parental rights being abandoned to the state.

These court rulings and judicial fiats are enough to give you a full picture of just how our public schools descended from their noble beginnings to their present state. Religion, morality, individualism, absolute truth, prayer, and the Bible are out, while Darwinian evolution, humanism, secularism, collectivism, and relativism are in. Public schools are not neutral on the subject of Christianity; they are hostile toward it (James 4:4). **How then can we send our children into schools that are designed to be devoid of Christ when we know that Christ said, "Let the children alone, and do not hinder them from coming to Me" (Matthew 19:14)?**

Nevertheless, "let not your heart be troubled" (John 14:1). Simply realize the truth about public schools, get your children out of them, and take hold of God's bright alternative in homeschool. I told you before that I hope you will see God's providential effects in these events, and I'm ready to tell you about the good side of them. In my next letter, I will give you a little more history – this time about the protection of parents' rights and the emergence of the homeschool movement. When you read my next letter, you will have reason to smile and marvel at the workings of God on behalf of His children. Until then, "be anxious for nothing, but in everything by prayer and supplication with thanksgiving let you requests be made known to God" (Philippians 4:6).

Regards in the Lord,
Stacey

10

Parents' Rights and the Return of Homeschooling

Dear Christian Parents,

In my last three letters, I have recounted to you how American public schools trended away from God until the courts finally removed the Christian religion from schools altogether. The current result of this trend is **a public school system which cannot cultivate faithfulness to God in your children.** However, I promised to give you reason to be optimistic, and now I am ready to bring you the good news. While the public schools were in a decline toward complete godlessness, there was another wave of legal rulings that remarkably trended in favor of parents' rights in the matter of education. With these two trends emanating from the same courts, it seems that God has providentially led Christians away from the degrading public schools and toward His original design for children's education, which is for parents to teach their own children (Deuteronomy 6:4-9).

In this letter, I want to briefly provide for you the relevant parts of some court decisions regarding parental rights and education. Some of these decisions are quite old, but they are on the records as precedents to protect your rights in homeschooling your children. It is always good to know your rights, and sometimes it is necessary to remind others of them as well. Under the United States Constitution, homeschooling has always been legal, but not all educational professionals, social workers, lawmakers, and judges are willing to concede to parents' rights. Consider the following comments by

Michael Farris, Chairman and General Counsel for Home School Legal Defense Association (HSLDA):

> Because the United States Constitution is the highest law of the land, homeschooling has always been legal in all 50 states...It has been a bit of a fight to get the various members of the education and social services establishment to accept that fact, but great progress has been made. Currently about two-thirds of the states have specific laws authorizing and regulating homeschooling. In the balance of the states, homeschoolers may legally operate as a small private school or provide "equivalent instruction." The details vary considerably from state to state and opinions about the law vary from district to district. What does not vary is HSLDA's commitment to the constitutional right to teach one's children at home.[57]

Before we consider the cases from the courts, I should explain the significance of categorizing parental rights as "**fundamental**." When a right is recognized to be fundamental by a federal court, it is considered to be virtually inviolable by government or any other party. The government may infringe on a fundamental right only when it can prove a compelling interest under a high level of scrutiny in court. Even when the government proves a compelling interest, it must use the least restrictive means possible to enforce that interest. On the other hand, rights that are not fundamental may be overridden by governments with only reasonable interests and without high levels of scrutiny.

I am happy to say that time and time again, the U.S. Supreme Court has recognized parental rights as fundamental, which you will see in the cases I will cite. As far as I know, the only significant exception to this is within public schools, where state and federal courts have ruled that parents abandon their rights when they enroll their children (see my last letter[58]). I will warn you that the fundamental status of parental rights is threatened by the fact that these rights are implicit rather than explicit within the Constitution. In

---

[57]Michael Farris' comments retrieved 7/13/11 from Home School Legal Defense Association website, www.hslda.org/earlyyears/BigQuestions.asp.

[58] See Chapter 9, "The Separation of Church and State."

other words, it has been understood by courts that parental rights are protected even though nothing in the Constitution states this outright. Usually, the Fourteenth Amendment has been the basis for courts recognizing these implied rights, but there is a danger of federal judges reversing precedents without an explicit provision for parental rights within the Constitution. This is the reason many Americans favor a parental rights amendment to the Constitution, which would explicitly define parental rights as fundamental.[59]

Now getting back to the court rulings pertaining to parental rights, the first case for us to notice is the U.S. Supreme Court's decision in *Meyer v. Nebraska* in 1923. The issue of this case was a Nebraska law restricting foreign-language education. In that decision, the Court stated, "Corresponding to the right of control, it is the natural duty of the parent to give his children education suitable to their station in life..."[60] Despite the universal presence of compulsory government schools by the date of this ruling, the court recognized parents as naturally responsible for their children's education.

Next, consider *Pierce v. Society of Sisters*, which was decided by the U.S. Supreme Court in 1925. In this case, the state of Oregon had amended the state's compulsory attendance law for public schools and eliminated the exception for children attending private schools. This was an attempt by the state to end parochial and Catholic schools. The Court built upon the principle it had previously stated in *Meyer v. Nebraska* by giving the following ruling:

> The fundamental theory of liberty upon which all governments of this union repose excludes any general power of the state to standardize its children by forcing them to accept instruction from public teachers only. The child is not the creature of the state; those that nurture him and direct his destiny, have the right, coupled with the high duty, to recognize and prepare him for added obligations.[61]

In essence, the Court was denying the state laws that compelled children to attend public schools in favor of parents' rights and du-

---

[59] See parentalrights.org.

[60] *Meyer v. State of Nebraska*, 262 U.S. 390 (1923).

[61] *Pierce v. Society of the Sisters of the Holy Names of Jesus and Mary*, 268 U.S. 510 (1925).

ties to provide for their children's education in any manner they saw fit. When the Court it said that a "child is not the creature of the state," it recognized that a child is strictly the responsibility of his parents.

In 1944, the U.S. Supreme Court issued another relevant decision for parental rights in *Prince v. Massachusetts*. The issue was whether a Watchtower Society member had violated child labor laws by having her nine-year-old daughter pass out literature on a street corner. In their decision, the Court stated, "It is cardinal with us that the custody, care and nurture of the child reside first with the parents, whose primary function and freedom include preparation for obligations the state can neither supply nor hinder."[62] This part of the Court's ruling recognized the inability of the state to prepare a child to meet his future obligations. It also recognized that the state must not hinder parents from providing such preparation. This was another victory for parents.

In 1965, the U.S. Supreme Court made a landmark ruling in *Griswold v. Connecticut* regarding the Constitution's protection of the right to privacy. In that ruling, the Court reaffirmed their rulings in *Meyer v. Nebraska* and *Pierce v. Society of Sisters* by saying, "...the right to educate one's children as one chooses is made applicable to the States by the force of the First and Fourteenth Amendments."[63] In this, the Court stood consistently on its previous opinions in upholding parents' rights. Specifically, the Court recognized parents' rights in the matter of education.

In 1972, the U.S. Supreme Court made several important rulings regarding parents' rights in *Wisconsin v. Yoder*. In this case, the Court upheld the rights of Amish fathers in Wisconsin to remove their children from compulsory school after eighth grade. The Court identified three deciding points for cases of this nature. These points are:

1. It must be shown that persons objecting to state law hold sincere religious beliefs that conflict with the law;
2. It must be proved that the state has interfered with the individual's religiously motivated conduct and thus interfered with his fundamental religious rights;

---

[62] *Prince v. Commonwealth of Massachusetts*, 321 U.S. 158 (1944).

[63] *Griswold v. Connecticut*, 381 U.S. 479 (1965).

3. If the first two points are proved, then it must be proved that the state's interest outweighs the individual's religious rights in order for the state to continue its interference.

This was a victory for parents because it has always been difficult for a state to prove that its interests outweigh an individual's fundamental rights.

A few important statements are found in the Court's opinion in *Wisconsin v. Yoder.* The Court stated, "The values of parental direction of the religious upbringing and education of their children in their early and formative years have a high place in our society."[64] It also made the following important historical observation:

> The history and culture of Western civilization reflect a strong tradition of parental concern for the nurture and upbringing of their children. This primary role of the parents in the upbringing of their children is now established beyond debate as an enduring American tradition.[65]

Finally, notice the following words written about a state's compelling interest by Chief Justice Warren E. Burger:

> Thus, a State's interest in universal education, however highly we rank it, is not totally free from a balancing process when it impinges on fundamental rights and interests, such as those specifically protected by the Free Exercise Clause of the First Amendment, and the traditional interest of parents with respect to the religious upbringing of their children so long as they, in the words of *Pierce*, "prepare [them] for additional obligations."[66]

All of this added up to good news for parents, for the Court recognized the fundamental rights of parents in the upbringing and education of their children.

For the sake of brevity, let me give you a few more important statements given in three other U.S. Supreme Court rulings.

---

[64] *Wisconsin v. Yoder*, 406 U.S. 205 (1972).

[65] Ibid.

[66] Ibid.

Our decisions establish that the Constitution protects the sanctity of the family precisely because the institution of the family is deeply rooted in this Nation's history and tradition. It is through the family that we inculcate and pass down many of our most cherished values, moral and cultural. (*Moore v. East Cleveland*, 1977)[67]

We have recognized on numerous occasions that the relationship between parent and child is constitutionally protected. (*Quilloin v. Walcott*, 1978)[68]

In a long line of cases, we have held that, in addition to the specific freedoms protected by the Bill of Rights, the "liberty" specially protected by the Due Process Clause includes the rights... to direct the education and upbringing of one's children. (*Washington v. Glucksberg*, 1997)[69]

Finally, in 2000, the U.S. Supreme Court made several important statements regarding parents' rights in *Troxel v. Granville*. In this case, the Court invalidated a Washington state law that permitted any third party to petition state courts for child visitation rights over parental objections. The Court said, "The liberty interest at issue in this case – the interest of parents in the care, custody, and control of their children – is perhaps the oldest of the fundamental liberty interests recognized by this Court."[70] It then made several references to previous rulings, including *Pierce v. Society of Sisters*, *Prince v. Massachusetts*, *Wisconsin v. Yoder*, and *Quilloin v. Walcott*, and concluded, "In light of this extensive precedent, it cannot now be doubted that the Due Process Clause of the Fourteenth Amendment protects the fundamental right of parents to make decisions concerning the care, custody, and control of their children."[71] At last, the Court determined, "The Due Process Clause does not permit a State to infringe on the fundamental right of parents to

---

[67] *Moore v. East Cleveland*, 431 U.S. 494 (1977).

[68] *Quilloin v. Walcott*, 434 U.S. 246 (1978).

[69] *Washington v. Glucksberg*, 521 U.S. 702 (1997).

[70] *Troxel v. Granville*, 530 U.S. 57 (2000).

[71] Ibid.

make childrearing decisions simply because a state judge believes a 'better' decision could be made."[72]

With all of these decisions raining down from the Supreme Court over the years and the public schools in shambles, conditions have become perfect for Christian parents to remember their first love. That has indeed happened, for different persons (not all Christians) through different paths began to arrive at the same conclusion: **thoughtful parents need to remove their children from the public schools.** Many chose private schools, but others saw that some of the same problems existed in private schools as were found in the public schools. Homeschooling began to emerge as a serious alternative to formal schools, and many books and magazines were published to make the case for homeschooling and to teach parents how to educate their own children. I will leave it to you if you want to research the work of persons such as John Holt, Dr. Raymond and Dorothy Moore, Ivan Illich, Charles E. Silberman, John Taylor Gatto, J. Rousas Rushdoony, Dr. Brian Ray, Michael Farris and the Home School Legal Defense Association (HSLDA), and many others who have had various roles in exposing the truth about public schools and advocating for homeschooling. Some of these were more spiritually-minded than others, but I am certain that the resultant reemergence of homeschooling in America is quite providential. Homeschooling has returned from near-extinction (about 13,000 students in the late 1970s), and now more than two million K-12 students were homeschooled n 2010.[73]

These last four letters have given you a lot to think about, so let me give you a simple summary. The education of children has historically been the responsibility of parents, and the same was true during the early history of America. The original intent of education in America was to promote religion, morality, and knowledge. Through the years, the public schools of America have been transformed from their noble beginnings, and now they are incapable of providing anything other than a secular humanist education for children. Thankfully, the practice of homeschooling has resurfaced

---

[72] Ibid.

[73] Brian D. Ray, "2.04 Million Homeschool Students in the United States in 2010," National Home Education Research Institute, 1/3/11. Retrieved 4/14/11, from www.nheri.org/HomeschoolPopulationReport2010.html.

as a strong alternative for Christian parents who want to provide their children with a God-centered, Bible-based education. This practice is not only legal, but it has been strongly defended many times in principle by the U.S. Supreme Court.

Now, it is your turn to render your own verdict. Is it good to send your children to public schools? Can your children attend public schools and learn to be God-centered with a Biblical worldview when God and the Bible have been eliminated from public schools? Is there a better alternative for Christians than homeschooling? You know my beliefs, but you will have to decide for your own family. In case you need more convincing, I have more to give. In my next two letters, I will focus a little more attention on the current state of public schools and the effect of government upon them.

Regards in the Lord,
Stacey

11

Complying with
The Government

Dear Christian Parents,

By now, you should share my concern over public schools. Over the last century, evolution and humanism have infiltrated the public schools, and the courts have cleared the path by enforcing their bogus application of the First Amendment in the schools via their errant interpretation of "separation of church and state." As a result, the religion and morality of Christianity have been replaced with the religion and *immorality* of humanism. For Christian parents to send their children into such an environment throughout their formative years and expect them to emerge as faithful Christians is unreasonable. This does not mean that it is impossible for a child to pass through public school without losing his or her faith, but the odds are very poor and the way is very difficult.[74] To borrow a figure from the Lord, it may be easier for a camel to go through the eye of a needle than for a public school student to be a Christian. "With men this is impossible, but with God all things are possible" (Matthew 19:26).

In my next letter, I want to further explain my concern about public schools. I don't mean to beat a dead horse, but there is much more that you need to know about the issues. Besides, the public schools are not what I would call a dead horse. Instead, they

---

[74] See the studies by the Nehemiah Institute and by Dr. Robert Simonds cited in Chapter 6, "No Greater Joy."

are a fire-breathing dragon that needs to be slain. I don't mind beating on them a little bit more.

Before I go any further in deriding public schools, which are government schools, I want to use this letter to clarify that I am not suggesting that you or I should be defying the government in any way. It is the will of God for the benefit of all people that we all subject ourselves to the governing authorities. According to Romans 13:1-7 and 1 Peter 2:13-17, the authorities that exist are established by God, and whoever resists such authority opposes the ordinance of God. "Rulers are not a cause of fear for good behavior, but for evil." The authority established by God in government "is a minister of God to you for good." Government officials are sent "for the punishment of evildoers and the praise of those who do right." The God-given scope of government from these passages is very simple – to encourage good behavior and to punish evil. Therefore, God-fearing, law-abiding Christians need not fear the government as it does its God-given work. They simply must comply with all laws that apply to them, including those that compel their children to attend school.

However, Christians must also apply wisdom and discretion to God's mandates pertaining to any government of men. In this way, we must "be shrewd as serpents and innocent as doves" (Matthew 10:16). In the case of education laws, homeschooling is a legal alternative to compulsory government school in every state of our nation, so Christians may shrewdly and innocently comply with the authority of government through this godly alternative. Of course, laws concerning homeschooling vary from state to state, and Christians must abide by the state laws wherever they live. Nonetheless, no one in the United States is currently required to surrender his or her children to the government for education, for even the U.S. Supreme Court has declared, "The child is not the creature of the state" (*Pierce v. Society of Sisters*, 1925).[75]

Speaking of state homeschooling laws, I cannot overemphasize the importance of knowing and complying with the laws of your particular state. If you choose to homeschool your children, then it is absolutely essential that you do the research to find what is required of you in your state. The differences in laws from state to

---

[75] *Pierce v. Society of the Sisters of the Holy Names of Jesus and Mary*, 268 U.S. 510 (1925).

state make it impossible for me to explain in this letter what you must do where you live, but there are resources that you can check to find out for yourself. Most states have homeschool associations or organizations that can give you up-to-date information for complying with the state government, so you may want to use an internet search engine and find such a group for your state. You may also check with one of the homeschool legal service organizations, such as Home School Legal Defense Association (HSLDA) or Homeschool Legal Advantage (HLA). I do not recommend asking your local board of education or any public or private school personnel about homeschooling laws because it is simply not their expertise.

Now getting back to the issue of a Christian's submission to government, it is very important for us to recognize that the order of authority in any government begins with Almighty God, and our first allegiance is always with Him – "God reigns over the nations, God sits on His holy throne" (Psalm 47:8; see also 2 Chronicles 20:6). Government is established to be "a minister of God to you for good" (Romans 13:4), but if government becomes a minister of evil, then it fails in its God-given purpose and becomes illegitimate by the higher law of God. Such a corrupt government will not stand for long (Psalm 9:17), but while it continues, Christians who are subject to it must deal with its evil ways with shrewdness and innocence.

Even with a very good form of government such as we have in the United States, if a law made by men requires us to violate God's law, then we must not comply with that law of men. Let us look to history and consider the godly men and women who defied the ungodly statutes enacted by their governing authorities. The book of Exodus tells us of Shiprah and Puah, the Hebrew midwives who feared God and disobeyed the Egyptian king's commandment to put the Hebrew sons to death (Exodus 1:15-22). In the book of Daniel, we read of Shadrach, Meshach, and Abed-nego, who refused to serve Nebuchadnezzar's gods in spite of the king's command (Daniel 3), and Daniel, who continued to pray to God in defiance of Darius' decree (Daniel 6). In the New Testament, when the apostles were commanded by the Sanhedrin to stop preaching Jesus, Peter said, "We must obey God rather than men" (Acts 5:29; see also Acts 4:19-20). Non-Biblical sources tell of many other faithful persons who have resisted rulers in the name of God and suffered for it. These godly men and women defied their rulers and accepted any punishment they had incurred, but they refused to compromise in their commitment to God.

Like those who have righteously defied human rulers before us, we must also be unwavering in our allegiance to God and ready to suffer any consequences of our commitment to Him. To support this point, notice 1 Peter 3:13-16:

> Who is there to harm you if you prove zealous for what is good? But even if you should suffer for the sake of righteousness, you are blessed. And do not fear their intimidation, and do not be troubled, but sanctify Christ as Lord in your hearts, always being ready to make a defense to everyone who asks you to give an account for the hope that is in you, yet with gentleness and reverence; and keep a good conscience so that in the thing in which you are slandered, those who revile your good behavior in Christ will be put to shame.

Perhaps we can fulfill this passage by having a ready answer for our coworkers or neighbors who might ask us about our beliefs, but the real meaning of this passage in context is that we should be ready to stand trial before the governing authorities who have the power to do harm to us. Just as we would make a defense of ourselves in a court of law if we were wrongfully accused of a heinous crime, so also we must defend our hope in Christ with reverence before any authorities who require us to give an account. The key to success in such a situation is to "sanctify Christ as Lord in your hearts." He is our Lord and ultimate authority, and our undivided allegiance must be to Him regardless of the decrees of men.

The principle of God's preeminent authority is vitally important for the protection of our children. Christian fathers have a stewardship from God whereby they must "bring [their children] up in the discipline and instruction of the Lord," (Ephesians 6:4) and Christian mothers are required by God to love their children and likewise bring them up (1 Timothy 5:10; Titus 2:4). If adherence to any government statute would cause fathers and mothers to violate their sacred trust and stewardship, then they must resist and seek for a godly alternative. Thankfully, we have a godly alternative to compulsory government schools that allows us to spare our children from the evil influences found in those schools and maintain our sacred trust and stewardship before God.

Remember that the Lord Jesus said, "Render to Caesar the things that are Caesar's; and to God the things that are God's" (Matthew 22:21). Jesus was speaking specifically of our responsibility to pay taxes to the government, but we can make an important application to our children. Whereas our money bears the images of Caesar (i.e. government), our children bear the image of God (Genesis 1:26-27). Therefore, our children do not belong to Caesar, but to God. Christ said Himself, "Let the children alone, and do not hinder them from coming to Me; for the kingdom of heaven belongs to such as these" (Matthew 19:14). There is never a time under any government to yield our God-given parental rights and responsibilities to governing authorities and hinder our children from coming to the Lord. Historically, there have been times when godly parents had to save their children from governing authorities – Jochebed saved Moses from Pharaoh (Exodus 1:15-2:10), Joseph and Mary saved Jesus from Herod (Matthew 2:13-18) – and those times have come to us as well. Our government does not seek to kill our children (federal funding for abortion notwithstanding), but the government schools do seek to indoctrinate them with human- ism and Darwinian evolution, which will lead our children away from the saving faith of Christ's gospel.

Christian parents, let us understand that we have a pressing re- sponsibility to our God, our children, our nation, and our govern- ment. We are commanded to pray for "all who are in authority, so that we may lead a tranquil and quiet life in all godliness and dig- nity" (1 Timothy 2:2). By answering our prayers through His own providence, God will provide for us the "tranquil and quiet life" that we seek for our families. It is then our responsibility to live "in all godliness and dignity" in every way, including in the way we teach our children. God has blessed us with a great liberty in this nation to educate our children in His ways, and we must take hold of the opportunity with both hands. "Act as free men, and do not use your freedom as a covering for evil, but use it as bondslaves of God" (1 Peter 2:16). This is not a time to abuse our freedom for our own selfish pleasures, but rather it is a time to live for Christ and work for our children's temporal and spiritual future. Our children, our nation, and our government will be better for it. "For such is the will of God that by doing right you may silence the ignorance of foolish men" (1 Peter 2:15).

In my next letter, I will get back to beating that dead horse and slaying that dragon. When I do, please keep in mind the principles that I have set forth in this letter. May God bless you, your family, and the United States of America with God-fearing citizens and leaders.

Regards in the Lord,
Stacey

12

Government Schools
And the NEA

Dear Christian Parents,

I told you in my last letter that it is necessary for Christians to comply with any laws that govern them, including those that compel their children to attend school. I also told you that Christians should use discretion, wisdom, shrewdness, and innocence when complying with the laws of men. **In the case of compulsory school laws, the discreet, wise, shrewd, and innocent way for Christians to comply is to avoid the public schools altogether and educate their own children at home.** This is the best way for Christians to keep their children out of the corrupted public school system, and, thanks to God, it is legal in all fifty states of our nation.

In this letter, I want to give you a little more insight into the current state of our public school system and where it may be going in the future. I believe that the more you know about public schools, the more you will want to keep your children away from them. Of course, I have told you many times that my goal is to convince you to educate your children in the best way to cultivate faithfulness to God within them, and that goal is partly achieved by convincing you that public schools are a great detriment to your children's faith in Christ. I have shown you in previous letters that evolution and humanism are the driving forces in the public schools, but there is much more that you need to know. Some of the information I want to share with you is temporal in nature, and some of it is spiritual, but all of it is important for you to know.

To start, let's understand that public schools are now government schools. Of course, you know this already, but I want you to think about how modern government schools (state funded and controlled schools) are different from the public schools (schools open to the general population) of the past that were run by parents and local communities. Government involvement in modern schools has led to predictable results, for many years ago, James Madison said, "The essence of Government is power; and power, lodged as it must be in human hands, will ever be liable to abuse."[76] As government expanded its power into all aspects of education, the public schools were affected with a plague of abuses that are not easily cured. As a parent, you need to be aware of these problems.

I explained some of the history of public schools in previous letters[77], but consider now the transformation of public schools from a functional standpoint. When the state and federal governments took over the management of public schools, all the trappings of government management entered the schools. All of the characteristic ineptness of government institutions, such as the Department of Transportation, is found in the public schools. Likewise, all of the intimidation, regulation, and fraud of the IRS are also found in the public schools. Worse still, all of the political correctness and social experimentation that are forced onto government entities such as the armed forces are also found in the public schools. The public schools themselves are probably the worst example of government waste, for as of 2009 more than $11,000 per student per year is spent on public education in America with continually diminishing results.[78] The performance of government institutions is generally so poor and inefficient that the phrase "close enough for government work" has become a cliché to describe the low expectations and subpar results in government enterprises. With all of that said, do you really want to trust your child's education to the government?

---

[76] James Madison, Speech at the Virginia State Convention, December 2, 1829. Retrieved 4/14/11 from the Constitution Society website, www.constitution.org.

[77] See Chapter 7, "The Original Intent for Education in America," and Chapter 8, "Common Schools, Evolution, and Humanism."

[78] U.S. Department of Education, National Center for Education Statistics. (2010). *Digest of Education Statistics*, 2009 (NCES 2010-013) Table 180 and Chapter 2. Retrieved 4/14/11 from the National Center for Education Statistics website, nces.ed.gov.

One reason that government management is so bad for public schools is the many layers of bureaucracy that stand between the students and the main decision makers. Starting at the top with the U.S. Department of Education, each layer of bureaucracy presents more opportunity for bad and even evil policies, irrelevant decisions, corruption, and waste. Moreover, the managers at the top of the bureaucracy are so far removed from the students that their decisions are badly out of touch with the real needs of the students and their parents. Not only are they out of touch, but they do not care to get in touch, for they consider parents to be ignorant and unqualified to make decisions about their children's education. Instead of seriously consulting parents about their children's schools, state and federal departments of education turn to so-called experts and education professionals for guidance. These experts and professionals are very biased with ideas and agendas that are extremely detrimental to students. The government officials that make policies on education take the ideas and agendas of the experts and professionals and force local public school systems to implement them by means of monetary incentives, manipulation, and intimidation.

The modern model of government management in the public schools is a far cry from the old days when teachers were selected by the community in which they worked to teach to the needs of their particular students. The old model of community management for public schools made good sense, for it allowed the parents to be directly involved in their children's education, whether it was in hiring teachers, determining curriculum, academic expectations, scheduling, or anything else. Just as the Lord designed a local church to be managed locally by elders who are within that local church (Acts 20:28; 1 Peter 5:2), a local school is best managed by the people within that locality. Unfortunately, the days of community management of schools are long gone.

Academically, government schools have been an abysmal failure. Take for example a comparison of the literacy rates in America from before compulsory government schooling and today. At the time Horace Mann and Massachusetts passed the first compulsory school laws in 1852, illiteracy rates among American children and adults were around 10 percent. After more than 150 years of government-led education, the illiteracy rates in many public schools range from 30 to 70 percent.[79] The failing techniques of public schools, such as the "whole language" or "look-say" method of reading instruction, threaten to send children back into the Dark Ages of illiteracy that the early American colonists sought to escape. Granted, there are many factors that play a part in this failure, but there is no excuse for such performance in the public schools. John Taylor Gatto, who taught in New York City public schools for over thirty years and was named New York State Teacher of the Year, estimates that a willing child can be taught to read, write, and do basic arithmetic in about one-hundred hours.[80] Before compulsory schools, parents had no trouble teaching these basics to children, but now government schools often fail to do this in twelve years. As I said, there is no excuse for this.

Government administration of public schools also carries a significant portion of the blame for the steep decline in morality in our nation. Remember that the original purpose for public schools in America was to teach religion, morality, and knowledge. While it may appear that the government has gotten schools out of the business of teaching religion and morality, it really hasn't. Christian religion and Bible-based morality have been removed, but they have been replaced with the religion of humanism and the morality of relativism. Public schools now teach "values clarification," which is a method of imparting subjective morality to students. The United Nations Educational, Scientific, and Cultural Organization (UNESCO) explains **values clarification** by saying:

> Values guide our decisions as to what is good, true and right. Thus, they depend as much on our feelings as on our thoughts. Values clarification is a technique for encouraging students to relate their thoughts and their feelings and thus enrich their awareness of their own values.[81]

The result of such teachings is a culture of people whose morality has no objective standard, for each person has been told to

---

[79] Joel Turtel, *Public Schools, Public Menace: How Public Schools Lie and Betray Our Children*, (New York: Liberty Books, 2004-2005), pp. 12-16.

[80] John Gatto, *Dumbing Us Down* (Philadelphia: New Society Publishers, 2005), p. 12.

[81] Retrieved 7/16/11 from the UNESCO website, www.unesco.org.

decide "what is good, true, and right" according to his feelings. Public schools have taught them to do what is right in their own eyes (Judges 17:6; 21:5; Proverbs 12:15). In other words, they have been told, "If it feels good, do it." This is humanism 101, and it has resulted in an increasingly immoral society.

Another reason that government management has ruined public schools is the massive amount of money involved. Education is enormous business. According to the National Center for Education Statistics, public school districts spent $562.3 billion on education in 2007, which was 4% of the entire gross domestic product of the United States.[82] For the 49.3 million students enrolled in public schools that year, there were 3.2 million persons employed as teachers and millions of other persons employed as administrators and staff personnel. Any time that much money and that many people are bound up in one enterprise, there is going to be trouble, "for the love of money is a root of all sorts of evil" (1 Timothy 6:10).

Money wasn't a problem in the former days of public schools, for communities paid their teachers directly at their own expense. They also built schoolhouses at their own expense, or else the students and teachers assembled in church buildings or even houses. Unlike those former times, hundreds of billions of dollars are now spent every year in education for consistently poor results, and yet politicians constantly make campaign promises of more money for education. Why?

The big business aspect of government education means that one of the primary purposes of modern schools is to provide jobs, and the primary concern of school employees is to make an income. Public schools are lauded as benevolent institutions that exist strictly for the welfare of the students, but that simply is not the case. There is nothing wrong with seeking employment and profit, but when attendance in public school is forced by law and the means of funding public education is mandated by the government, there are major conflicts. Public education has become a government-run monopoly, and the people in charge of the monopoly seek to destroy any threat of competition. It is in these types of situations that the government becomes that abusive power of which James Madison spoke.

---

[82] *Digest of Education Statistics*, 2009.

From the standpoint of parents, there is also a business and money aspect of government schools. For most parents, the offer of free education is virtually irresistible. The fact that public schools are free often overwhelms any incentives parents might have for seeking better education for their children that might cost them money. In fact, many parents become dependent on the free schools so that they cannot function without them. In this way, free schools have become like an addictive drug, and the government is the drug dealer. The government picks up the children in the morning, does all the work of teaching them and watching over them, and then returns them when the day is over – for free! This allows the parents to do whatever they want to do during the day, including working to make more money. What could be better than free babysitters (schools, I mean) and more income? Who can resist such an offer?

Economically, government schools appear to be a great blessing for parents and children. The public school system seems too good to be true – and it is. This free education costs tax payers more than half a trillion dollars per year and spiritually ruins most of the children it takes in. The truth is that the government schools need the children in order to justify the taxes required to fund their massive business. Public education markets itself as a free product, and the public believes it because they have to pay the same taxes whether they have children in the government schools or not. However, these schools are far from free, and their expense is much more than just the money required to support them.

In contrast to the big-business government schools, parents who homeschool their children are only concerned with their children. For them, their children's education will never be a matter of money, business, or profit. Christian homeschool parents' sole agenda will never be anything other than the spiritual, physical, and mental wellbeing of their children. This facet of homeschooling alone makes it vastly superior to all formal schools, whether they are public or private.

An organization that embodies and propagates all of the problems with compulsory government schools is the **National Education Association (NEA)**, which is the main labor union that represents teachers and other educational professionals in the public schools. The NEA is the largest labor union and the largest professional organization in the nation. It is an absolute beast of a union, a powerful influence in schools, and a forceful lobbying group in Washington, D.C. and state capitals around the nation. As a union, the NEA's only legitimate function should be to negotiate for suitable wages and working environments for its members, but the NEA overreaches those boundaries and forces itself into every aspect of education. The NEA has the most input into the government school curriculum, and it passes radical resolutions that often become policies in the government schools. The leaders of the NEA are the so-called experts and education professionals that I mentioned before who guide the state and federal departments of education.

The influence of the NEA is so devastating to government schools and the students because their agenda is absolutely anti-Christian. With the massive influence that they have, their evil agenda has a disastrous effect on our nation's children. To get an idea of this agenda, consider a small sampling of the NEA resolutions from 2009-2010:[83]

- Resolution A-34 states the NEA's opposition to "federally or state-mandated choice or parental option plans." In other words, they do not want parents to have any alternatives to government-run public schools. I believe the reason for this is that the NEA desperately wants to remove children from the influence of parents and to eliminate their competition. If this resolution resulted in law, then home-schooling would become illegal.

- Multiple resolutions are made that associate homosexuality (categorized as "sexual orientation") with traits such as race, gender, disability, and ethnicity. This is an attempt to normalize homosexuality as a natural, acceptable, and unchangeable characteristic rather than a voluntary behavior that defies the laws of God (Leviticus 18:22; Romans 1:26-27; 1 Corinthians 6:9-11).

- Resolution B-1 declares support for "early childhood education programs" in the public schools beginning at birth. The NEA wants federal legislation requiring these programs from birth, including "mandatory kindergarten with compulsory attendance." The NEA wants to get their hands on

---

[83] 2009-2010 NEA Resolutions. Retrieved 9/8/09 from the NEA website, www.nea.org.

your children as soon as they are born because this would mean more NEA jobs and more opportunity to indoctrinate children. For the children, it would mean the loss of the precious early years of godly training with their parents. This idea is pure communism, for Karl Marx's closest associate, Friedrich Engels, described one necessary measure of communism as "All children will be educated in state establishments from the time when they can do without the first maternal care."[84]

- Resolution B-51 declares that public schools must be involved in sex education. The recommended sex education program includes instruction concerning birth control, family planning (a code term for abortion, as in "Planned Parenthood"), "diversity of culture and diversity of sexual orientation and gender identification" (to teach homosexuality and sexual deviancy), and "homophobia" (to teach children not to believe homosexuality is sinful or immoral).

- Resolution I-16 declares support for "family planning, including the right to reproductive freedom." The NEA urges "the government to give high priority to making available all methods of family planning to women and men unable to take advantage of private facilities." It also urges "the implementation of community-operated, school-based family planning clinics that will provide intensive counseling by trained personnel." All of this is about the abortion of unborn children, which the NEA favors very strongly. The murder of innocent children is a detestable abomination to God (Proverbs 6:17; Exodus 21:22-25; Deuteronomy 12:31), but this is of no concern to the NEA. Of course, it seems that more births would mean more children for the NEA to prey upon, but it is really a matter of eliminating those children whom the NEA leaders find less desirable. (To this point, I recommend looking into the origin of Planned Parenthood and its founder, Margaret Sanger. I

---

[84] Friedrich Engels, "Draft of a Communist Confession of Faith," from MECW Volume 6, p. 92; written by Engels, June 9 1847; first published in *Gründungsdokumente des Bundes der Kommunisten*, Hamburg, 1969, in English in *Birth of the Communist Manifesto*, International Publishers, 1971. Retrieved 7/13/11 from the Marxists Internet Archive, www.marxists.org.

hope you have a strong stomach because it is a sickening story.)

- Resolution I-32 invokes the Supreme Court's interpretation of "separation of church and state" for the First Amendment. The NEA opposes prayer in schools, for they will not even tolerate observances of moments of silence. They claim to favor the teaching of religious heritage in the history of our nation, but in truth their actions show that they are absolutely opposed to Christianity's influence in schools.

NEA resolutions such as these inevitably end up as policies in departments of education and become mandates in government schools. Because the NEA steers the government schools, you can read their present resolutions and see where the government schools are going in the future.

When I read the NEA's plans for government schools, they remind me of *Brave New World* by Aldous Huxley, who was a twentieth-century humanist author. So many of the elements of that story are now advocated by the NEA, such as government control of children from birth, the teaching of sexual promiscuity and birth control, the advocacy for immorality and godlessness, etc. If these are the intentions of the NEA and the state and federal departments of education, then instead of homeschool there will be school-home where every child is turned over to the government from birth to be raised by the state. Schools truly will become the "alma maters" (Latin for "nourishing mothers") of our children, for they will serve as parents.

This Brave New World is closer than we may want to imagine, for the NEA is lobbying for the ratification and implementation of a treaty that could create a Brave New World in the United States and around the world. This treaty was adopted by the United Nations as international law in 1989, and it is called the Convention of the Rights of the Child (CRC). Despite its noble-sounding title, the CRC is a Trojan horse and a wolf in sheep's clothing that is designed to take away parental rights and supplant them with government control. The NEA favors the CRC because it would significantly expand their power and influence over children. Consider a few of the provisions of the CRC:[85]

- Article 2 requires that the rights set forth in the CRC will override any religious, political, or cultural beliefs of a child or his or her parents.

- Article 6 of the CRC requires the "State Parties" (government, U.N.) to ensure the development of the child. It is the government, not the parents, who are to "develop" children.

- Article 12 requires that a child be allowed to express views and make his or her own choices with no provision for parents' approval.

- Article 14 mandates the child's right to "receive and impart information and ideas of all kinds" with the parents' rights respected only as long as they provide direction "in a manner consistent with the evolving capacities of the child." Of course, the appropriateness of parents' direction and the "evolving capacities of the child" are to be determined by the U.N. states.

- Article 14 also limits religious rights according to what is "necessary to protect public safety, order, health or morals, or the fundamental rights and freedoms of others." Again, these necessities are determined by the U.N. For example, if the U.N. decides that Christianity's teachings about homosexuality put homosexuals' rights or freedoms in danger, then children could be prevented from learning Christianity.

- Article 17 encourages "the mass media to disseminate information and material of social and cultural benefit to the child" as determined by the U.N. This article mandates that a child must have "access to information and material from a diversity of national and international sources, especially those aimed at the promotion of his or her social, spiritual and moral well-being and physical and mental health." This means that if the government decides that a child should be

---

[85] "Convention on the Rights of the Child." Retrieved 4/14/11 from the Office of the United Nations High Commissioner for Human Rights website, www2.ohchr.org/english/law/crc.htm.

exposed to something his or her parents consider objectionable, the parents have no right to interfere. Notice that this article requires diversity in the areas of spirituality and morality, which means that the government can demand that your child be taught the Koran or any other religious information.

As I write this, 194 nations have ratified the CRC, but the United States has not. The only other member of the United Nations that has not ratified this treaty is Somalia, and this may be the only time in history that it is good to be in agreement with that nation. However, officials within the United States government have indicated that they intend to ratify the CRC, and the pressure is on. Thanks to the NEA, the CRC may soon become a reality in the United States. If this treaty is ratified, then it will override any constitutional protections of parental rights.

I know this is scary stuff, but all that I have told you is true – it is not just paranoia or wild conspiracy theories. The NEA leaders even admit their own corruption and self-serving goals. Consider the words of Bob Chanin, General Counsel for the NEA, who spoke of the effectiveness of the NEA during his retirement speech in 2009:

> Despite what some among us would like to believe, it is not because of our creative ideas. It is not because of the merit of our positions. It is not because we care about children. And it is not because we have a vision of a great public school for every child. NEA and its affiliates are effective advocates because we have power. And we have power because there are more than 3.2 million people who are willing to pay us hundreds of millions of dollars in dues each year because they believe that we are the unions that can most effectively represent them, the unions that can protect their rights and advance their interests as education employees.[86]

The reaction to these words was a standing ovation and wild applause by NEA members. This is an appalling example of the

---

[86] Bob Chanin, General Counsel for the NEA, retirement speech, 2009. Quoted by Neal McChuskey of The Cato Institute in "Retiring General Counsel's Shocking Admission: The NEA Is a Union!" 7/10/09. Retrieved 4/14/11 from www.cato-at-liberty.org.

unvarnished arrogance of this organization and their wicked agenda. At this point, they do not even attempt to hide their evil ways. The NEA even recommends that their members read Saul Alinsky's *Rules for Radicals*, a book that was dedicated to Lucifer by the author.[87] Need I say more?

These are the reasons that it is so important for you to get your children out of the government school system now, for these schools are already consumed with corrupt philosophies. The government-run public schools have become the primary mechanism for indoctrinating our children with humanism, immorality, and godlessness, and they are getting worse. Keeping our children out of their influence is a matter of heeding the words of our Lord in Luke 6:39-40:

> A blind man cannot guide a blind man, can he? Will they not both fall into a pit? A pupil is not above his teacher; but everyone, after he has been fully trained, will be like his teacher.

Please understand that for all that I have told you in this letter, the least of my concerns about public schools is inefficiency, waste, and money. My greatest concern is for the effects of the public school environment on the spiritual wellbeing of children. Please, save your own children while you can, and pray for other children that they might also be rescued.

In my next letter, I'm going to change gears to address one of the first questions that people typically have about homeschool: "What about socialization?" I have an answer that turns the argument back against compulsory schools. As you will see, socialization is one more reason to keep your children away from public schools and to teach them yourself. Until then, I urge you to keep pressing on for your children in the name of Christ.

Regards in the Lord,
Stacey

---

[87] Recommendation retrieved 4/14/11 from the NEA website, www.nea.org.

13

What About Socialization?

Dear Christian Parents,

By now, your eyes should be wide open to the goodness of home-based education for your children as well as the dangers of public schools. Nevertheless, I expect for you to have questions and maybe even objections. After all, I am asking you to make a radical change and commitment involving your children, so you should consider everything carefully and critically. If you are not sold on homeschooling yet, then I hope my next three letters will finish the job of convincing you by answering those questions and settling those objections.

I want to use this letter to address the most common objection I hear regarding homeschooling, which is that homeschooling does not provide adequate socialization for children. The term **socialization** is used to describe the process of acquiring values, beliefs, and interactive skills found among the group of people in which one lives (society). The socialization objection to homeschooling arises from the fact that homeschool students are not usually immersed into a large population of children in the way that public and private school students are. The concern is that homeschool students will lack the opportunities to interact and communicate with other children, and therefore they will be rendered socially awkward and unprepared to function in society as adults.

First of all, let me state that homeschooling does not require withdrawal from society. Socialization is important, and homeschoolers are concerned about this for their children just like any other parents. God has said that it is not good for man to be alone

(Genesis 2:18), so all people, including children, need to have relationships with others.

God's first provision for this need was marriage and the family (Genesis 1:27-28; 2:19-24), and homeschoolers recognize that this is still by far the best means of socialization. God did not supply Adam's social needs by creating a group of peers, but rather He made a wife for Adam and told them to be fruitful and multiply. This design is still the best provision for the social needs of both adults and children. **Daily interaction with parents, siblings, and extended family members will be more than enough to give children the social skills that God intended.** Marriage and family are the most basic and important building blocks of society according to God's design, and homeschooling embraces that design while much of the world attempts to destroy it.

Beyond family relationships, most homeschoolers that I know keep their children engaged with other children and adults in various ways. They participate in homeschool groups, co-ops, field trips, play-dates, clubs, sports, visitation, Bible study groups, church, etc. If you make the decision to homeschool, then you may choose for your children to engage in as many social activities as you deem appropriate. How much time your children spend with others and who those others are will be completely up to you, so you should have no concerns regarding homeschooling and socialization.

Now let's take a moment to challenge the implied assumption that the socialization of formal school is somehow superior to that of homeschool. Supposedly, the great advantage of formal school with regards to socialization is that children in formal school are constantly interacting with many other children. In other words, children allegedly learn good social skills in formal schools by learning from other children. I do not dispute that children learn from one another, but I do not see how they can possibly learn good (emphasize *good*) social skills in this way. Think about it: do children learn to have manners, confidence, courtesy, kindness, grace, honor, maturity, poise, tact, or any other good social skill from other children? **Rather than learning good social skills from other children, a child can only learn more childish behavior.** Therefore, it is preposterous to suggest that mere membership in a classroom of twenty or thirty other children that are all the same age will instantly prepare a child with the social skills he will need to function as a mature Christian adult.

According to the Scriptures, the correct way for children to learn social skills (or anything else) is through interaction with godly adults rather than with other children. This point is made well by considering the first part of **Proverbs 22:15 – "Foolishness is bound up in the heart of a child..."** along with **Proverbs 13:20 – "He who walks with wise men will be wise, but the companion of fools will suffer harm."** Let's put these passages together and make an application with regards to the topic of socialization. Our children will obtain wisdom by socializing with wise men and women. On the other hand, our children will actually suffer harm by socializing with other children in whose hearts foolishness is bound.

Do not misunderstand this: I am not suggesting that God has forbidden children from playing together. I am saying that when it comes to socialization and education, homeschooling fits the Biblical pattern much better than formal schooling. In homeschooling, children get the very best socialization of all, which is the constant, loving companionship of wise, godly parents and those whom their parents choose to be good influences. Ask yourself: who can better teach your children how to interact and communicate with others – you, or a classroom full of children?

Someone may object to my assertions by saying that children actually do learn lessons in courage, problem solving, sharing, compromising, and other similar social skills when interacting with other children. I concede that children experience for themselves the goodness and truth of these lessons when they apply their own good social skills with others, which is why children should interact and play together. However, children do not learn these social skills from one another, but rather they learn them from their parents or other adults. Untrained and undisciplined children will usually solve their social disagreements by manipulation, intimidation, or violence. In other words, they will bribe, mock, dare, lie, threaten, scream, hit, bite, pull hair, etc. to get their own ways. On the other hand, children who have been trained properly in godly social skills by their parents will experience the goodness and righteousness of those lessons when they apply them with other children.

The reality of socialization in formal schools can actually be quite ugly. When I think of my own experiences in the public schools, I cannot identify a single good social skill that I acquired. However, I can think of many bad social skills that I learned (and had to unlearn). If you don't believe that public school socialization will be a bad influence on your children, then let me offer a few questions to give you a proper perspective on the issue. (This is where the public restroom comparison from my fifth letter is very astute.) **Exactly what are the social skills that you fear your children will be missing if they do not attend public schools?** Are you worried that they won't learn all the curse words? Are you troubled that they won't learn to ridicule people for their clothes, weight, disabilities, etc. or that they won't get to be the victims of such ridicule while they are young and vulnerable? Are you afraid that they won't get beaten up or that they won't get to beat up other children? Are you concerned that they won't get exposed to lewd talk, filthy jokes, so-called "alternative lifestyles," or even pornography before you teach them about godly relationships between men and women? If by age thirteen your child is not a zombie with his mind swallowed up by some portable high-tech gadget, will you be disappointed in his development? I know this kind of socialization is not what you had in mind for your children, but this is the essence of public school social skills. As far as I'm concerned, if the lack of such social skills makes my children socially awkward, then so be it.

It is because of corrupt socialization that many children hate attending formal schools. Rarely is a child so intimidated by his teachers or so frustrated by his studies that he dreads going to school. In most cases, if a child dreads school, it is because of the other children. The constant misbehavior, ungodliness, abuse, and teasing found in formal school classrooms, hallways, restrooms, lunchrooms, and buses can make life miserable for a child. He becomes like Lot living in Sodom, who "by what he saw and heard that righteous man, while living among them, felt his righteous soul tormented day after day with their lawless deeds" (2 Peter 2:8).

Sadly, many parents and school administrators view the misery of such a child as a problem with that particular child rather than a problem with the formal school environment. While the child is trying to be separate (2 Corinthians 6:14-18), the adults expect him to adjust and assimilate to his godless surroundings. Many children beg their parents to get them out of this situation, but their pleas usually fall on deaf ears. Isn't it time that we start listening to these tortured souls and save them from despair? "What man is there among you who, when his son asks for a loaf, will give him a stone? Or if he asks for a fish, he will not give him a snake, will he?" (Matthew 7:9-10)

God's word warns of the harmful effects of bad socialization, and we need to take those warnings to heart in regards to our children. Notice this familiar passage from **1 Corinthians 15:33 – "Do not be deceived: bad company corrupts good morals."** I must say that I take no pleasure in describing any children as "bad company." I do not consider my children to be better than any other children, for all are children of the heavenly Father who created them in His image (Genesis 1:26-27; Ephesians 4:6). It breaks my heart that so many children are corrupted from their God-given innocence at such young ages by the trash and filth of the world (1 John 2:16). This is not the fault of the children, but rather it is the fault of the parents who allow their children to be exposed to corrupting influences. Regardless of whose fault it is, many public school students have learned wickedness that I do not wish to be shared with my children. Sadly, these public school students have become the "bad company" that will corrupt the good morals that you and I are instilling in our children. Of course, we would like to think that we can prepare our children so well that they cannot be corrupted, but we must not be deceived. The right course of action is to keep them away from the bad company.

By the way, if you are thinking that your children's good morals might win over the bad company they might encounter, then think again. Your children are not missionaries, and the school is not a mission field. Your children are just that – children. They are not yet equipped with the maturity, experience, and knowledge to take on the kinds of temptations that they are likely to encounter in the public schools (see Galatians 6:1). Neither are they ready to endure the persecution that is likely to come to them when they attempt to teach Christianity to their schoolmates. Not only are they likely to receive the mockery of other children, but also they may be punished or even suspended by school authorities.[88] It is a noble and godly instinct to desire help for other children who are not be-

---

[88] Bill Bumpas, "PJI not tolerating school's 'diabolical' actions", OneNewsNow, 4/5/11. Retrieved 4/5/11 from www.onenewsnow.com.

ing raised in the discipline and instruction of the Lord, but your young children are not the right instruments for this job. Again, the Scripture says it best: "Do not be deceived: bad company corrupts good morals."

I know all of this may seem pessimistic and cynical, but it isn't. Instead, it is honest, realistic, and practical. You have to be defensive when you are a parent. The pressure of the masses that will come on your children in formal schools is powerful, and you need to protect them from it. Ralph Waldo Emerson was right when he wrote, "You send your child to the schoolmaster, but 'tis the schoolboys who educate him."[89] Those "schoolboys" will have at least as much input into your children's education as their teachers will have. There is a commandment in the Old Law of Moses that says, **"You shall not follow the masses in doing evil, nor shall you testify in a dispute so as to turn aside after a multitude in order to pervert justice" (Exodus 23:2).** This commandment acknowledged that universal temptation to do what everyone else is doing even when it is wrong. Some call this "peer pressure," and it gets stronger when there are more peers involved. One day your children will be grown and hopefully prepared by your diligent training to face this pressure, but don't make them face it before they are mature enough to overcome it.

Realize now that you have such a wonderful opportunity to bless your children by giving them godly associations and keeping them from ungodly socialization. Consider **Psalm 1:1 – "How blessed is the man who does not walk in the counsel of the wicked, nor stand in the path of sinners, nor sit in the seat of scoffers!"** How blessed your children will be not to walk in the counsel of the wicked, nor stand in the path of sinners, nor sit in the seat of scoffers because they will be at home with you. Please don't deny them this tremendous blessing.

Remember that for Christian parents the goal of their children's education should be to cultivate faithfulness to God in their children. In contrast to that, the humanists' goal for education is to achieve societal transformation by removing God from society. Which goal do you think is likely to be achieved by socialization in

---

[89] Ralph Waldo Emerson, essay "Culture" from "The Conduct of Life" (1860, rev. 1876). Retrieved 4/14/11 from www.emersoncentral.com.

modern, godless, humanistic public schools? In Psalm 119:9, the Scripture asks a question: "How shall a young man keep his way pure?" The answer is not "by socialization," but rather it is, "By keeping it according to [God's] word." How can socialization in public schools help our young men and women to keep their ways pure when God's word is not even allowed in the schools?

In summary, my advice to you about socialization is not to be so much concerned about the quantity of socialization that your children receive, but instead you should focus on the quality. Notice **Proverbs 18:24 – "A man of too many friends comes to ruin, but there is a friend who sticks closer than a brother."** Seek those associations for your children that will help them to build up the Christ-like character that will serve them well throughout their lives. Homeschooling allows you to do this far better than formal schooling, and therefore socialization is a point in favor of homeschooling rather than against it.

And one other thing – if you are still worried about your children being socially awkward because they are homeschooled, then put your worries to rest. My experience with homeschoolers is that their children are the best behaved, most engaging, well-adjusted children that I ever meet. In fact, I can usually identify a homeschooling family almost immediately by the behavior of their children. There is a noticeable difference between a homeschooled child who knows how to communicate with people of all ages and a child from formal school who only knows how to communicate with children his own age.

In my next letter, I will continue this theme by considering whether sheltering your children from the world is harmful to them. Until then, keep studying, meditating, and praying about your children's education. May God bless you and your family.

Regards in the Lord,
Stacey

14

Is It Harmful to
Shelter Your Children?

Dear Christian Parents,

My last letter gave you some strong advice regarding socialization for your children, and now I want to briefly continue that discussion by posing a question. If you choose to follow my recommendations by educating your children at home, then will you shelter them too much for their own good? Obviously, I don't think so, or else I wouldn't have given the advice that I did. However, there are some who object to homeschooling because they consider it to be too protective, so let's talk about it.

The "sheltered life" objection asserts that homeschooling is harmful for children because it protects them from the world too much. The alleged harm comes from depriving children from formal school learning opportunities that build character and prepare them to cope with problems later in life. Without these opportunities, it is feared that children will grow up maladjusted and unable to handle conflicts, temptations, stress, and other adult situations.

I do believe that there can be too much sheltering for a child. Many life-lessons are best learned through experience, so children need those experiences as part of their development. Mistakes and consequences are great teachers through which children learn on their own. A few bumps, bruises, and scrapes along with moderate doses of embarrassment and regret will teach a child not to repeat behavior that produces unpleasant results.

However, I do not agree that homeschooling is too protective. Some parents may be overprotective, which is their prerogative, but that has nothing to do with homeschooling. Nothing about home-schooling requires for children to be deprived of character-building experiences that are appropriate for them. As I said in my last letter, homeschooling does not require withdrawal from society; it only requires withdrawal from formal schools. Homeschooling parents and children live in the real world just like everybody else, and their experiences are common. These children have ample opportunities to gain life experience and become prepared for adult life as their parents guide them.

This is not to say that homeschooled children are not protected, for they are in most cases. As I have written before, homeschool children are protected from all kinds of filth and trash along with the humanism and evolution that dominate the public schools. By preventing their children from being exposed to deceptive, persuasive, and seductive presentations of wickedness and evil, home-school parents protect the minds, hearts, and souls of their young ones from harm. How can that be a bad thing? I know of nothing in the Bible that speaks against sheltering children from evil influences. After all, the Lord taught us to pray to our heavenly Father, "And do not lead us into temptation, but deliver us from evil" (Matthew 6:13). Why would we not offer our children the same protection that we seek from our Father?

Remember that your children are an inheritance from God (Psalm 127:3-5; see my third letter), and as such they merit your protection. Your children are a holy treasure that others seek to rob, defile, and profane, so you must be proactive in keeping them safe. Notice what the Lord said in **Matthew 7:6 – "Do not give what is holy to dogs, and do not throw your pearls before swine, lest they trample them under their feet, and turn and tear you to pieces."** Jesus wasn't speaking directly of children, but we can certainly make an application to them, for our children are holy and of much greater value than pearls. If you don't protect your own children from the dogs and swine of this world, then no one will.

Even the ancient Greeks and Romans recognized the need to protect their children from harmful influences. The upper class families in these cultures would appoint their most trustworthy slaves to oversee the upbringing and morals of their boys. These slaves were the boys' constant companions until manhood, and the boys did nothing without the slaves' supervision (see Galatians 4:1-

2). The name for such a slave was *paidagōgos*, which literally means "child-leader" (translated as "tutor," "schoolmaster," and "instructor" in English translations of 1 Corinthians 4:15 and Galatians 3:24-25). If these pagan, idolatrous people were concerned about protecting their children from undesirable influences, then shouldn't Christians be at least as concerned for their children?

It is odd to me that the idea of sheltering young children from harm can be considered to be harmful itself. All parents understand the necessity of providing shelter for their children against the physical dangers – heat, cold, rain, wind, storms, etc. Why is it not also universally understood that children need just as much spiritual protection? You would never toss your five year old child into the freezing cold without adequate clothing and say, "He has to learn to deal with the world sooner or later." Why then would you cast him to the dogs in the public schools to face temptations that he is not prepared to handle? Somehow the world has turned this around so that highly attentive parents are considered to be harmful to children. It makes me think of this passage from **Isaiah 5:20 – "Woe to those who call evil good, and good evil; who substitute darkness for light and light for darkness; who substitute bitter for sweet and sweet for bitter!"**

If we look closely at the "sheltered life" objection to homeschooling, then we will see that there are at least two major errors in it. One error is that the objection assumes homeschool children will never be exposed to the world and its problems until they are adults. I will admit that this assumption is true in some ways, for homeschool children won't likely be exposed to pornography and similar garbage, but how can missing out on those things be harmful? As far as having exposure to character-building opportunities such as conflicts or trials, homeschool children may have as much exposure as their parents deem appropriate. As I have pointed out many times before in these letters, if you choose to homeschool, then you will make all the decisions for your children's education. **You will know best when your children are mature enough to take on tough situations and make the right choices.** You will introduce them to the world on your terms rather than someone else's terms. You won't shelter them from the world forever, but you will shelter them until they are ready.

Let me illustrate my point regarding this first error by using the topic of alcohol. The erroneous assumption would be that a homeschooled child would grow up in total shelter and complete un-awareness of the temptations and dangers of alcohol. He would then be so unprepared for the temptation of alcohol as an adult that he would be in terrible danger of succumbing the sin of drunken-ness. However, the reality of homeschooling is quite different. For example, my wife and I have taught our children about the evils of alcohol through the use of God's word and the real-life example of a man we know who destroyed his life in alcoholism. Our children know what alcohol does because we let them see it with their own eyes. Judge for yourself: is this a better way of teaching children, or is it better to leave them unsheltered so that they learn about alco-hol from some teenage public school student who got his informa-tion from movies and beer commercials on TV? Does the "shel-tered life" still seem like such a bad idea?

The other error of the "sheltered life" objection to home-schooling is the false assumption that the public schools are some utopian environment for building character in children. This as-sumption is so bad that it is almost comical to me. Not only does public school fail to build good character, but also it promotes many bad characteristics that I do not want my children to acquire (see my last letter). My goal as a Christian parent is to build godly, Christ-like character in my children (Philippians 2:1-8; 2 Peter 1:5-11; 3:17-18). What is there in the public schools that can possibly help achieve this goal? If anyone wants to convince me that there is a better way to develop my children's character than for them to be under my protection, then he needs to come up with a much better alternative than public schools.

The truth is that homeschooling is much better for preparing children to live as Christians (emphasize *Christians*) in this world than formal schooling could ever be. Adult Christians are not to constantly expose themselves to sin as a way of learning about it, so why should children be trained to do so? The Scriptures implore us to be separated (dare I say "sheltered"?) from evil, so why shouldn't our children be separated also? Consider a few passages of Scrip-ture to support this point:

> Thus says the LORD, "Do not learn the way of the nations..."
> (Jeremiah 10:2a)

...I want you to be wise in what is good and innocent in what is evil. (Rom 16:19b)

Brethren, do not be children in your thinking; yet in evil be infants, but in your thinking be mature. (1 Corinthians 14:20)

Do not be bound together with unbelievers; for what partnership have righteousness and lawlessness, or what fellowship has light with darkness? Or what harmony has Christ with Belial, or what has a believer in common with an unbeliever? Or what agreement has the temple of God with idols? For we are the temple of the living God; just as God said, "I will dwell in them and walk among them; and I will be their God, and they shall be my people. Therefore, come out from their midst and be separate," says the Lord. "And do not touch what is unclean; and I will welcome you. And I will be a Father to you, and you shall be sons and daughters to Me," says the Lord Almighty. (2 Corinthians 6:14-18)

But examine everything carefully; hold fast to that which is good; abstain from every form of evil. (1 Thessalonians 5:21-22)

One last thing – there is something about the "sheltered life" objection to homeschooling that reminds me of Satan's argument against Job. Notice the devil's accusations to God in Job 1:10-11:

Have You not made a hedge about him and his house and all that he has, on every side? You have blessed the work of his hands, and his possessions have increased in the land. But put forth Your hand now and touch all that he has; he will surely curse You to Your face.

I guess it is the implication that homeschooled children will either be crushed by the world or else will go wild once they leave the "hedge" of their parents' care. Of course, Job endured his trials with patience, and homeschooled children will do the same.

Lord willing, my next letter will attempt to answer a few more objections that some of you may have about homeschooling. For now, I hope that you will keep thinking on the things I have presented to you, and keep praying for God's guidance in your decisions.

Regards in the Lord,
Stacey

15

Are the Public Schools
Really That Bad?

Dear Christian Parents,

I have had much to say about public schools, and I anticipate that some of you still have objections, disagreements, or solutions that don't involve withdrawing your children from public schools. For this reason, I will use this letter to anticipate some of those responses and attempt to address them. My purpose in doing this is not to prove that I'm right and others are wrong, but rather it is to give you answers to help you make the best decisions for your children. Some of my answers to these issues have been given in my earlier letters, but I don't mind restating them in order to clearly connect the answers to the specific issues.

The first response I expect is simple disbelief. You might say, "The public schools cannot be as bad as you have described them." My reply to this statement is to say that everything I have told you about history, court rulings, the NEA, socialization, and the modern, godless state of public schools is true. You may check the references I have given for yourself or do your own research if you aren't satisfied. You will find that not only are the public schools generally as bad as I have described, but in many specific cases they are much worse. I have showed you merely the tip of the iceberg, and there is much more that I could show you. If you need more evidence regarding the poor academic and social performance of the public schools, then I suggest you read John Taylor Gatto's books or other similar resources that give honest, thoughtful evaluations of public schools. However, I am sure that your greater concern is for the spiritual hazards of public schools, and I have shown you that they are deadly dangerous to the souls of your children. Yes indeed, the public schools are that bad.

Another response might be suspicion. Maybe you are asking, "Why do you write so much about public schools when you are supposed to be writing about homeschooling?" Perhaps you think I cannot build a strong enough case in favor of homeschooling, and therefore I have redirected my efforts to tear down public schools. I assure you that this is not the case, for my first six letters could stand alone upon the foundation of the Bible even if every mention of public schools was removed from them. The reason I have written so much about public schools is because nearly 50 million children in America attend them, including most children from Christian families. I could not address the subject of education to Christian parents without talking about the compulsory schools that are pulling in most of your children like a massive black hole in space. You need to know what the public schools are doing to your children and that homeschooling is a godly shelter from this calamity.

There are also various forms of denial. Perhaps you accept that there are problems in the public schools, but you deny that they will cause any lasting harm to your children. You might say, "We can correct any errors taught to our children." For example, if the schools teach your children that man slowly evolved over millions of years, then you will simply counteract that teaching with the truth of Genesis 1. That sounds easy enough, but how will you know when your children have been taught such falsehoods? They can't report to you everything they have learned in school, and they can't know which lessons were false in order to ask you to correct them. Even if you could somehow detect every ungodly influence exerted on your children, you are still outmatched. You will make a grave error if you expect to counteract an entire program of education that is designed to teach your children a completely secular, godless way of understanding the world. The daily exposure to humanist indoctrination that children must endure for twelve years of public school leaves a mark that is not easily erased. Day by day, their capacity for faith will be eroded, and in the end they will be branded with a hot iron that scars them for life.

Another form of denial is to see your family or your schools as the exception. In this case, you might say, "These things won't happen to my children," or, "Our school is different." Granted, some schools are better than others, but every modern American public school is fundamentally flawed by design. I remind you again of this quote from the book *Humanism: A New Religion*: "Education is the most powerful ally of Humanism, and every American public school is a school of Humanism."[90] That book was written in 1930, and the influence of humanism in public schools has increased beyond measure since then. Regardless of where you live in the United States, the public schools in your community will not cultivate faithfulness to God in your children. They will not teach anything about the true and living God in any part of their curriculum because federal law forbids them to do so. On the other hand, they will teach secular humanism because federal law requires them to do so. They will also teach Darwinian evolution explicitly and implicitly. Your children and their schools will not be exempt from these rules.

It is also possible for you to deny the problems if you are too close to be aware of them. If you have been immersed in the public school system for years as a student, an employee, or even a parent, then you may be so accustomed to the ways of public schools that you cannot perceive of even their most blatant flaws. Many Christians who are involved with the public schools daily have lost the ability to see the influence of evolution and humanism in the schools because they have been indoctrinated themselves. They have been led to believe that the absence of Christianity in schools is evidence of secular *neutrality* rather than secular *humanism*. Yet no one can be neutral about Jesus, for He taught, "He who is not with Me is against Me; and he who does not gather with Me scatters" (Matthew 12:30; Luke 11:23). The public schools are certainly not with Jesus, for their students and teachers cannot even talk about Him. Likewise, the schools' curriculum are not spiritual in any way, so they must be founded solely on human wisdom (ref. Matthew 21:25; Mark 11:30; Luke 20:4). Therefore, modern public schools are secular humanist institutions by nature.

---

[90] Charles Francis Potter, *Humanism: A New Religion* (New York: Simon and Schuster, 1930), p. 128. Cited by David Limbaugh, *Persecution: How Liberals Are Waging War Against Christianity* (New York: HarperCollins Publishers, 2004), p. 65. Retrieved 7/13/11 from books.google.com.

If you cannot see the problems of public schools because you are too involved in them, then I want to help you gain some perspective. Try to look at the schools with a purely Christian mindset. Open your eyes and ears on a spiritual level, and consider both what is present in the schools and what is absent from them. Present in the public schools are subtle, implicit, and sometimes disguised forms of humanistic indoctrination. They never use the term humanism, but they teach it just the same. Examples of such indoctrination are:

- The training of children to look to men in government and science for answers to all of life's questions and solutions to all of life's problems;
- The emphasis on socialization, collectivism, multiculturalism, self-esteem, and positive mental attitude;
- The teaching of reverence for "mother earth" and the animals, plants, trees, oceans, etc.;
- The provision of so-called "sex education" in which children are given the knowledge, tools, and implicit permission to become promiscuous or even homosexual.

Absent from public schools is any trace of genuine Christianity, such as:

- The reverent and truthful use of God's name;
- Any mention of the Bible as a source of truth;
- The teaching of the Bible's creation account even as an alternative possibility;
- Any notion of God's providence in the affairs of men;
- Any semblance of the Lord's discipline and instruction.

By law, Christianity has been erased from the public schools so that no one is allowed to speak of the Lord or to consider God's word as an answer to anything. This is the spiritual truth about public schools, and this perspective should prove to you that the problems I have described are real, serious, and abundant.

Another response to the things I have written in these letters may be misunderstanding. Some persons may honestly ask, "Why does a Biblical worldview matter for subjects like grammar?" It is true that subjects such as grammar or math are the same for every person regardless of religious beliefs, so these subjects can be taught in a universal way without much impact on a person's worldview. However, it is much better for believers in Christ to learn all things with a Biblical worldview. If we can teach our children grammar or math while also teaching them spiritual lessons, then shouldn't we do so? Short pieces of literature, sample sentences in grammar, and word problems in math make good places for stashing Scriptural messages and little bits of godly wisdom. I have told you many times that my goal is to convince you to educate your children in the best way to cultivate faithfulness to God within them. If grammar, math, or any other subject can be taught to your children in a way that inspires their faith in God, then they should be taught that way, for the fear of God is the beginning of wisdom, understanding, and knowledge (Psalm 111:10; Proverbs 1:7; 9:10). Of course, the public schools are not permitted to teach godliness in any way, but they do often teach unbiblical worldviews by hiding ungodly messages in grammar and math lessons.

Many people are fiercely defensive of public schools and are not very receptive to criticism such as I have given. Sometimes these defenses are honest and sincere, sometimes they are emotional responses, and sometimes they are attempts to justify a practice that is in error. I will not attempt to discern the thoughts and intentions of your heart, for only God can do that (Hebrews 4:12). However, if you are moved to defend the public schools against what I have said, then I ask you to evaluate your own motivation to see whether it is honest and true to the word of God. Answer for yourself: what exactly is your motivation? You may have a good answer, but here are some answers that are not so good:

- If you spent your entire academic career in public schools as I did, then you may be motivated by a strange affection for them. You may be affected by Stockholm syndrome, which is a psychological condition in which hostages develop positive feelings for their captors. (I'm joking a little bit, but not much.)

- If your children are already in public schools, then you may be looking for justification for keeping them there only for the sake of convenience.

- If you are employed by the public schools, then your motivation may have more to do with your job than with the wellbeing of your children and the truth of God's word.

- If you are simply afraid to plunge into homeschooling, then you may letting your fear cloud your good judgment and stop you from doing what is needed.

If you find that any of these is your motivation, then I urge you to change your mind, trust in God, and simply do what is right. Of course, I know that you will.

If you still disagree with me, then I respect your opinion. I only hope that you have sound, Scriptural reasons for your disagreement. If you still aren't sure, then I encourage you to err on the conservative side and keep your children at home. That may seem like a radical decision rather than a conservative one, but the weight of Scriptural proof is on the side of homeschooling. Your children's future is at stake, so your decisions about their education must not be made lightly. None of us can afford to be wrong when it comes to our children. May God guide us all.

Regards in the Lord,
Stacey

16

Private Schools and Colleges

Dear Christian Parents,

In these letters, I have had much to say about public schools but very little to say about private alternatives. I also have omitted any advice regarding colleges from my previous letters because it simply wasn't in the scope of my message. Therefore, I want to use this letter to briefly address private schools as well as colleges and universities.

Unlike public schools, private schools are difficult to evaluate as a single category. This is because there is so much variation from school to school. Of course, there are also variations in public schools, but most of the opinions I have given in these letters about public schools are based on the traits that they all share in common (state and federal government control, laws and court rulings that do not apply to private schools, socialization, etc.). Without as many common traits among private schools, I cannot give the same kind of blanket assessment for them as I did for public schools.

However, I do have some thoughts about private schools to share with you. If you have read my earlier letters, then you know that my intention is to convince you to homeschool your children instead of sending them to formal schools. A private school is a type of formal school, so I hope to convince you to choose home-schooling even over private schooling.[91] This is because I do not accept the notion that any formal school, whether public or private, can provide the same godly education that you can provide for your

---

[91] For definitions of formal schools and private schools, see Chapter 2, "Change Your Mind," or the glossary.

own children in your home. My opinion in this matter is based on the pattern for educating children that is given in the Bible[92]. As I have stated repeatedly in these letters, homeschooling is simply the best method of education for producing faithfulness to God within your children.

If I have failed to convince you to take the plunge into home-schooling, then I encourage you to search out the best private school available to you. The purpose of your search should be to determine which school, if any, will best promote and protect faith-fulness to God within your children. This means that you will need to carefully research and evaluate the available private schools on the basis of their conformity with God's word.

Assessing a private school will not be easy for you. To begin, you must not assume that because a school is privately operated it is necessarily better than the local public schools. Many private schools use the same godless curricula used in public schools and follow the public school agendas. Oftentimes, such private schools are actually more effective than public schools in teaching the pub-lic school doctrine. Therefore, beware of trading a dysfunctional public school in exchange for a more efficient private version of the same thing.

Because you are Christians, you will likely be looking into so-called Christian schools, but use great caution. Use of the name "Christian" in the description or title of any school means nothing if the school does not teach the word of Christ or operate on the principles of Christianity. Even among schools that make claims to Christianity, many of them use secular materials that have been de-veloped for public schools without the inclusion of God. Like public schools, these private schools teach godless history, godless literature, and godless science. Such schools are Christian in name only and lack the real substance of Bible-based education.

Be aware of any denominational connections that may influence the private Christian schools you consider. Most Christian schools are operated or at least affiliated with particular church denomina-tions, and those schools will teach the peculiar doctrines of their denominations. If you do not believe that a denomination teaches Scriptural doctrine, then you will want to avoid that denomination's

---

[92] See Chapter 4, "Looking for a Pattern."

private schools for your children's sake. Replacing the godless error of public schools with some denominational religious error is not the educational alternative your children need.

In general, Christian schools will be better for your children than public schools by a wide margin, but don't assume that the improvement is enough to cultivate sincere Christian faith in your children. In an earlier letter, I described the PEERS (politics, economics, education, religion and social issues) testing performed by the Nehemiah Institute to evaluate worldview understanding in young people.[93] I told you that the results of those tests show that 85 percent of public school students from families professing Christianity do not hold a Biblical worldview. Those same results also show that very few similar students from so-called Christian schools have a Biblical theism worldview.[94] Moreover, the year-to-year scores on those tests show that students of traditional Christian schools are trending away from a Biblical theism worldview at about the same rate as their public school counterparts.[95] Essentially, students from Christian schools are just a few years behind those from public schools in rejecting a Christian worldview. Compare these results to the findings of Dr. Brian Ray, whose studies show that you have a 94 percent chance of passing your religious beliefs on to your children when you homeschool.[96] Are you sure you won't reconsider homeschooling?

Whether you choose homeschooling or private schooling, I'm certain that you are also concerned about your children's college education. If you haven't given much thought to college, then I urge you to begin now. The time for you and your children to decide about college will be upon you faster than you realize, so start planning today.

The first thing you need to realize about college is that it is not genuinely necessary for all people to become college graduates.

---

[93] See Chapter 6, "No Greater Joy."

[94] Josh McDowell, *The Last Christian Generation* (Holiday, FL: Green Key Books, 2006), p. 14.

[95] "PEERS Trend Chart" by the Nehemiah Institute, Inc. Retrieved 4/14/11 from www.nehemiahinstitute.com and www.worldviewalliance.com.

[96] Brian D. Ray, *Home Educated and Now Adults*, (Salem, OR: NHERI Publications, 2004), pp. 60, 63, 71, 83.

That seems patently obvious to me, but governments and universities have promoted the myth that a college degree is indispensable for life in the United States. Unfortunately, most parents, students, and employers have believed this myth, and so the myth has become a kind of self-fulfilling prophecy. Because employers now have over-inflated expectations for their employees' college training, parents and students go to great extremes to satisfy employers' demands. Usually, this results in mountains of debt that place students into bondage before they even get their first job (see Proverbs 22:7). It also means a grossly inflated market for colleges and universities that is unaffordable despite heavy subsidies from tax-payers. All of this could be avoided if parents, students, employers, governments, and universities would be reasonable about what is really necessary and stop wasting time, effort, and money on unneeded college training.

Despite the strong opinion I just expressed, I am not at all opposed to college education. For certain professions, college training is absolutely necessary to perform the work. For other professions, a college degree is necessary for getting hired but not for doing the job. Either way, if a college degree is required for your child to get or to do the job he wants, then he will have to find a way to obtain that degree. You and your children will have to carefully evaluate each potential career choice to determine whether a degree is needed, whether it is a worthwhile pursuit, and, most importantly, whether it is an honorable and godly occupation.

If you and your children do resolve to pursue college degrees, then you must be extremely cautious how you do so. When you step into the realm of colleges and universities, you enter a minefield of spiritual danger that threatens to destroy everything you have worked to achieve in your family's homeschool. It would be counterproductive and contradictory for you to homeschool your children for the godly edification of their souls only then to give them over to the training of godless and humanistic professors for their college education. Likewise, it would be foolish and blind to protect your children from ungodly socialization throughout their early years only then to turn your young adults over to be influenced by fornicators and drunkards. Yet this is exactly what you will be doing if you follow the status quo by sending your young men and women to most state and private university campuses. If your goal in homeschooling is to educate your children in the best way to cultivate faithfulness to God within them, then I beg you not to allow others to destroy the results of your family's work in the name of college education. While not intending to advocate for families, Woodrow Wilson probably gave Christians the best warning of the dangers of college when he said, "The use of a university is to make young gentlemen as unlike their fathers as possible."[97]

I feel compelled to warn you of the dangers that come with college education and campus life so that you will be able to make informed decisions. Regarding education itself, you may have read before that higher levels of education correlate to lower levels of faith among high school and college graduates. Countless studies have been conducted that attest to this fact, but I find fault with those studies because they are misleading. The spiritual danger is not in the amount of education attained, but rather it is in the kind of education. Naturally, if young adults are immersed in the influence of humanism, evolution, and godlessness on college campuses, then their faith will likely be eroded as they become more educated in such things. However, if they are educated in God's word, honorable studies, and truly objective sciences, then their faith will actually flourish as they increase in education. Therefore, beware of the typical godlessness of many state and private universities, and seek out those institutions that offer their services with the fear of God.

Regarding campus life, I probably don't need to tell you what happens at most colleges because their reputations precede them. College campuses, fraternities, and sororities have long been associated with wild excesses of drunkenness and fornication, but the degree to which sin is now normalized in these places is absolutely stunning. For example, a recent Stanford University study of 17,000 students from twenty different colleges and universities found that 72 percent of both sexes had engaged in at least one act of fornication while in college. That statistic is appalling enough, but it is even worse than you may think. The particular act of fornication under consideration in the study is something called "hooking up," which is an arranged meeting that is strictly for fornication between virtual strangers. There are even internet-based

---

[97] Woodrow Wilson, "Address at the Young Men's Christian Association (YMCA) Celebration" in Pittsburgh on October 24, 1914.

services to facilitate such activity on college campuses. Now think about that number again – 72 percent of students surveyed reported this behavior, with an average of 9.7 encounters for men and 7.1 for women.[98] How can we Christian parents possibly consider sending our young adults into such environments and even paying a great expense to do so?

I hope you understand that I am not implying that your young adult sons and daughters cannot cope with the spiritual dangers of college, but I am suggesting that you choose the best path to help them maintain their purity, faith, and godliness. If you have home-schooled your children and instilled in them a genuine faith in Christ, then they are better prepared than anyone else to face these dangers. However, do not underestimate the power of temptation on college campuses, and do not overestimate your son's or daughter's willingness to resist. The Bible implores our young people to "flee youthful lusts" (2 Timothy 2:22), but if we parents go to great effort and expense to place them in college environ-ments of intense youthful lusts, then how difficult we have made it for them to flee. Let us not be guilty of putting them in situations that cause them to stumble (see Matthew 18:6-9). If a particular college campus is a likely place for our children to fall into sin, then let us keep them far from it. I am simply asking you to very soberly consider whether it is wise to send your young man or young woman into such an environment. Is it what God wants you and your children to do?

I'll wrap this up by saying all of us Christian parents need to be smart about any choices we make about college. One of the best options available to us today is online colleges, which bypass all of the drawbacks of campus living, usually at less expense. This doesn't mean that there are no dangers involved in online colleges, but the risks are significantly reduced. This is just one smart choice pertaining to college, and here are a few more random smart thoughts to consider for college:

- Don't buy a Rolls-Royce when a Ford will do. By that, I mean that there are many professions where a degree from a "Harvard on the Highway" is just as good as an Ivy League

---

[98] Sharon Jayson, "More college 'hookups,' but more virgins, too," USA Today, 3/31/11.

education, so don't become smitten with a university just because it has name recognition.

- If your children can get college credits without taking classes, then by all means have them do so. If they can get credit for high ACT or SAT scores, then take those credits. Let them take CLEP (College Level Examination Program) tests for credit. Have your young adults do whatever they can ethically to make it easier on themselves.

- Don't spend a fortune paying for a college degree that has few or no prospects for gainful, godly employment. Spending $100,000 for a degree that fetches a $25,000 salary makes no sense.

- If you and your young adult are interested in a theological degree, then be careful about your choices. There are liberal schools of theology, divinity schools, and seminaries that will actually do much more damage to a person's Christian faith than even humanist universities will do. Stay away from them.

- If your son's aptitude is more vocational, then don't force him into pursuing a four-year college degree. There are plenty of good vocational schools and even some apprenticeships available to young men who are willing to work. It is a noble and godly thing for a man to work with his hands, and many, many men support their families very well doing so.

- If your daughter's godly ambition is to be a wife, mother, keeper of her home, and teacher of her children as it should be, then help her pursue the skills that she will need to fulfill that ambition rather than pushing her to get a professional degree for the sake of worldly esteem. I'm not suggesting that young women should not be college educated, but rather that their education should match their true ambition.

- Don't forbid your sons or daughters from marrying for the sake of college. If he or she has found a godly person for a spouse, then let them be married. Godly marriage is much more important than any college degree. Besides, there is no reason why they cannot be married while they pursue college education.

- Neither you nor your children should go into debt for college. As I said before, debt is slavery (Proverbs 22:7), and college is simply not worth going into bondage. Many college students graduate with amazing amounts of debt that financially cripples them for years. Even worse, some don't graduate at all and still have student loans to pay off. Instead of taking on debt, pay as you go. Work and save the money, and don't send your children to college until you and/or they can pay cash.

By no means have I presented everything you need to know about private schools and colleges, but I hope the information I have given you helps you make wise, godly decisions. It is never my intention to make you feel discouraged, but rather I seek to encourage you in what is best for your children while discouraging you from poor choices. I know that you will make the right choices for your family and that God will bless you for it.

Regards in the Lord,
Stacey

Part III – My Appeal Applied

17

A Plan for Homeschooling

Dear Christian Parents,

Hopefully by now, you can see that homeschooling is the right educational choice for your family because it is the best way for you to cultivate faithfulness to God in your children. You have seen that your children are a precious inheritance from God entrusted to your stewardship, that your children's education is your God-given responsibility, that homeschooling is an excellent fit for the Biblical pattern of children's education, that your godly home is the best place for your children's education, and that teaching your children to walk in the truth is the key to your greatest joy as a parent. You have also seen the truth about government-run public schools, which are in no way equipped to produce faithfulness to God in your children. You know that the public schools can only tear down your children's faith and replace it with godless humanism. You also know your parental rights in the education of your children, which are limited by the government in the public schools but are limited only by God in your homeschool. If you were concerned about socialization, then your concerns have been relieved, for you now know that the godly social skills your children will learn in your home will be far superior to any worldly social skills they would learn in public schools. You have seen that the evidence favors homeschooling in every way, so I hope that you have reached the right conclusion.

Maybe you are convinced that you should homeschool your children, but you are intimidated by the idea of such a huge undertaking. That is understandable, for when you decide to homeschool, you are committing yourself to years of very hard work. It can seem overwhelming at first, but let your mind be at ease. When you endeavor to pursue godliness in any venture, you can have confidence of success because you are assured of the help of Almighty God. Take on the attitude of David, who wrote, "Behold, God is my helper; the LORD is the sustainer of my soul" (Psalm 54:4), and the psalmist, who said, "The LORD is for me; I will not fear" (Psalm 118:6). Remember the words of Paul, who wrote, "I can do all things through Him who strengthens me" (Philippians 4:13). This attitude of trust, faith, and confidence in God is exactly the right starting point for your homeschool.

Your confidence to homeschool your children will increase when you remember that God equips parents for the job of raising children and that the education of children is really just a natural part of that job. I demonstrated this truth to you in my third letter.[99] The reason homeschooling seems so daunting to modern parents is that they have somehow lost touch with much of their natural ability to raise children. I have read that chicken breeders have bred the brooding instinct out of hens so that they will lay eggs and abandon them voluntarily, and it reminds me of many modern parents. Just like those hens, it seems that we have bred the parenting instincts out of fathers and mothers so that they will bear children and voluntarily turn them over to the state for education. It is time for all of us to undo that unnatural breeding and get back in touch with our parental instincts. As you prepare to homeschool your children, consider it as a time to reclaim the natural abilities that God has given you to teach your own children.

To help you get started in homeschooling, I want to go back to some of the general guidelines from the Scriptures regarding the education of children. Recall again the Biblical pattern for education that we studied in my fourth letter.[100] We need to take a closer look at these important instructions. Knowing that these directions have come from God Himself, you should commit yourself and your children to them. As long as you follow God's plans in your homeschool, you can be confident that you and your children will have great success. "All your [children] will be taught of the

---

[99] See Chapter 3, "Nobody Else's Business."

[100] See Chapter 4, "Looking for a Pattern."

LORD; and the well-being of your [children] will be great" (Isaiah 54:13).

Let's notice again the plan God made for the education of Israel's children in Deuteronomy 6:4-9. This passage of Scripture comes from the Law of Moses, which is not binding upon Christians (Acts 15:10; Galatians 3:23-26; Colossians 2:13-14), but it is a divinely wise and effective source of guidance for anyone who is seeking to know the mind of God. This passage from Deuteronomy is the best text for summarizing the Biblical pattern for children's education that all Christians would be wise to follow. If you want to know how God would have the children of His people to be educated, then Deuteronomy 6:4-9 has the answer you seek. Consider the text of this passage:

> Hear, O Israel! The LORD is our God, the LORD is one! You shall love the LORD your God with all your heart and with all your soul and with all your might. These words, which I am commanding you today, shall be on your heart. You shall teach them diligently to your sons and shall talk of them when you sit in your house and when you walk by the way and when you lie down and when you rise up. You shall bind them as a sign on your hand and they shall be as frontals on your forehead. You shall write them on the doorposts of your house and on your gates.

This passage describes how the generation of Israel that was receiving the promised land of Canaan was to pass on their godly heritage to the following generations. For our own benefit, we can break down this text into a step-by-step set of directions and use it as an excellent plan to follow for homeschool.

The first step in God's plan for educating children is for parents to get their hearts set on God. The plan shows that in order to be effective, godly teachers of children, parents must first have an all-encompassing, personal love for God. This is the most important qualification of godly parents and for all Christians, for Jesus quoted from this very passage and identified the love of God as "the great and foremost commandment" (Matthew 22:37-38). This love starts with an unwavering commitment to the God of the Bible as the only true and living God and the only God who is to be served (compare to the first two of the Ten Commandments in Exodus 20:3-6). Furthermore, this love is manifested when those who love God keep His commandments, for Jesus said, "If you love Me, you will keep My commandments" (John 14:15; see also 1 John 5:3). Parents who truly possess and demonstrate the love of God are well prepared to succeed in educating their children, for they will pass on their love of God to their children. "A pupil is not above his teacher; but everyone, after he has been fully trained, will be like his teacher" (Luke 6:40). Remember that Dr. Ray's study found that 94 percent of homeschooled children retain the religious beliefs of their parents.[101] If you love God, then your home-schooled children will love God also.

The second step of this plan for education also concerns parents' hearts, for Moses said, "These words, which I am commanding you today, shall be on your heart." It is vitally important that parents have a firm understanding of God's word in their minds and a sincere dedication to God's word in their hearts. Of course, this commitment to God's word should be found in all Christians, for under the covenant of Christ, God has written His laws into the minds and onto the hearts of all His people (Hebrews 8:10-11). However, there are many persons professing to be Christians who know very little of the Bible because they have not studied it sufficiently (2 Timothy 2:15). Any Christian parents who are deficient in their knowledge of the Bible or their practice of God's word will be unprepared to educate their children in the ways of godliness. Such parents are unable to teach God's word to their children because they need to be taught themselves (Hebrews 5:12). Therefore, Christian parents who wish to homeschool must be serious about learning and keeping the word of God lest they act as blind guides of the blind (Luke 6:39).

Because you are faithful Christians, I trust that your hearts are already filled with a sincere love for God and a profound respect for His word. If so, then you are already living according to the first two steps of this plan, and you are ready to teach your children. The next step in the plan of Deuteronomy 6:4-9 is to set your heart on what you intend to teach them. According to God's words given by Moses, the parents in Israel were required to teach their children all of the words that God had commanded them. The

---

[101] See Chapter 6 – "No Greater Joy."

same requirement holds true for us Christians – we are to teach our children all of God's word, which now consists of both the Old and New Testaments. You should resolve right now to make the Bible the foundational textbook for your homeschool. The words of God that are stamped on your heart will govern everything that you teach your children.

Because you have the love for God and the respect for His word in your heart, I have no doubt that you see the importance of teaching the Bible in your homeschool. However, you may be wondering about subjects such as math, history, science, etc. – how do these fit into the plan from Deuteronomy 6:4-9? To answer this question, let's consider all that was entailed in Moses' words to Israel. When Moses directed the parents of Israel to teach their children all the words he commanded them, he spoke with reference to the Law given to them by God. Within that Law were words concerning religious matters, such as the priesthood, sacrifices, worship, etc., but there were also words concerning history, civil government, warfare, morals, business, marriage, family, children, and other diverse topics. If we consider all of the words of Moses contained in the five books he wrote (Genesis, Exodus, Leviticus, Numbers, and Deuteronomy), then even more subjects are involved. Moses' words even included the Genesis accounts of the world's creation, the global flood, and the tower of Babel, which are our foundations for understanding the sciences, such as biology, astronomy, geology, and anthropology. The words of Moses addressed everything the parents of Israel needed to teach their children, and likewise we now have the entire Bible to give us "everything pertaining to life and godliness" (2 Peter 1:3). Just as it was in Israel, God's word is still the basis for understanding everything in the world, and it must be the foundation of every subject you teach to your children.

To view everything through the lens of the Bible is to have a **Biblical worldview,** and this is the way that God would have you to teach your children. This means that every subject in your homeschool should be taught from a Bible basis, for "the fear of the LORD is the beginning of wisdom, and the knowledge of the Holy One is understanding" (Proverbs 9:10). In other words, reverence and knowledge for God are crucial for all learning, and therefore the Bible is indispensible in all education.

Teaching with a Biblical worldview may seem like a natural and easy choice for Christians, but it may be harder than you realize. If you attended public schools as I did, then you may have the residual effects of public school secularization. This can cause you to divide your thinking into two compartments – one secular and the other religious. In the secular compartment, you may think of math, science, most history, language arts, etc. In the religious compartment, you are basically left with the Bible, morals, and a small amount of history. We must overcome this compartmentalized thinking and integrate all subjects into one Biblical worldview. Secular thinking must be put away, for each Christian is commanded, "Set your mind on the things above, not on the things that are on earth" (Colossians 3:2; see also Philippians 4:8). There is no place in the Christian mind for worldly, secular thinking. Be aware that many writers of textbooks and homeschool materials think in these secular/religious compartments, so seek out material that teaches from a genuine, Biblical worldview.

Of course, not every detail of every subject can be found within the Bible, but that should not prevent us from teaching every subject with a Biblical worldview. For example, the Bible has almost nothing to say about mathematics, yet math can be taught with a Biblical viewpoint. This is done by showing that math is a way of expressing and communicating certain truths and natural laws, all of which have their origins in the God of the Bible, the Creator of the world. Therefore, you can teach your children that "1+1=2" is true because Almighty God made it true. This kind of approach to teaching can be used in everything. History can be taught with a providential emphasis, for God rules in the affairs of men (Psalms 66:7; 103:19; Matthew 5:45). (I will give a thorough explanation for teaching history in a future letter.[102]) Science can be taught with a view to God's creation, His natural laws, and the fact that Christ currently "upholds all things by the word of His power" (Hebrews 1:1-3). Any subject can be taught through a Biblical worldview, and this should be your method of teaching in your homeschool.

The last step in the plan of Deuteronomy 6:4-9 stresses the manner in which parents are to teach a Biblical worldview. The plan calls for parents to immerse their children in the word of God

---

[102] See Chapter 19, "Teaching History."

through diligence, repetition, and constant exposure. From the time the family wakes up in the morning until they go to bed at night, the word of God is to be read, spoken, and practiced. This means that your homeschool will always be in session, for opportunities for teaching can and will arise at any minute of the day. This also means that your homeschool will go wherever your family goes, whether you "sit in your house" or "walk by the way." In this way, your homeschool will provide your children with a deep, meaningful, and complete education in the word of God and a Biblical view of the world that will be nearly unshakeable.

Now that we have studied through this plan for our children's education, let's summarize the four steps:

Step 1 – Parents must love God with all their heart, with all their soul, and with all their might.

Step 2 – Parents must have the word of God stamped on their hearts.

Step 3 – Parents must teach their children the word of God and a Biblical worldview.

Step 4 – Parents must teach their children with diligence, repetition, and constant exposure to the word of God.

If you follow this plan in your homeschool, then you and your children will be wonderfully successful and tremendously blessed. Just as God promised to bless Israel for following His plan (see Deuteronomy 11:18-21), so also He will bless you.

With this general plan in place, you will be able to work out the details of your homeschool little-by-little as you go. Don't be overwhelmed by the prospect of teaching your children for twelve years, for you only have to teach them one day at a time. Likewise, don't be overwhelmed by all of the homeschooling curricula on the market, but find good Bible-based material that conforms to the purpose of your homeschool. You can even make your own material if you are inclined to do so. As long as you stick with your basic plan, you will do well.

I hope you found this letter to be encouraging and informative. It is my sincere desire to help you do the best thing for your family according to God's will. Lord willing, in my next letter I want to look at the topic of early education for your little children.

Regards in the Lord,
Stacey

18

Head Start Homeschooling

Dear Christian Parents,

Now that you have a good, Bible-based plan for conducting your homeschool, you are ready to put that plan into action. Why not get started right now? There is no time like the present to begin educating your children regardless of how old your children are. Of course, I know that you have been teaching your children many things already, but now it is time for you to put it all together and give your children the complete, God-centered education that they need.

In this letter, I want to concentrate on the subject of teaching the very youngest children. Whether we classify these children as babies, toddlers, or preschoolers, all of them need to be taught by their parents every day. Remember that the crux of your home-school plan is based on Deuteronomy 6:7 – "You shall teach [God's words] diligently to your sons and shall talk of them when you sit in your house and when you walk by the way and when you lie down and when you rise up." Notice that this commandment from Moses' Law placed no limits upon the ages of the children who were to be taught. Therefore, even the youngest children can and should be immersed in the word of God.

In ancient Israel, the children were introduced to the word of God almost from birth, and that precedent serves as a good pattern for us to follow today. In those old times, not only did the parents teach God's word to young children, but also their children were present whenever the people of Israel assembled, whether it was for the giving of the covenant (Deuteronomy 29:10-15), the reading of the Law (Deuteronomy 31:10-13; Joshua 8:33-35), the seeking of

God's help (2 Chronicles 20:4, 13; Ezra 10:1), or the worship of God (Joel 2:15-17). Among the children present in these assemblies were "nursing infants" (Joel 2:16) and "little ones" (Joshua 8:35; 2 Chronicles 20:13), which we would now call toddlers. (The term "little ones" is translated from the Hebrew word *taph*, which referred to the clumsy steps of small children.) Moses commanded the Israelite parents to bring their young children to hear the reading of God's word because "their children, who have not known, will hear and learn to fear the LORD your God" (Deuteronomy 31:13). Today, if we Christian parents would have our children to learn the fear of God, then they also need to hear the word of God from their earliest ages.

However, many Christian parents fail to give their young children a proper exposure to the word of God. A mentality exists among some Christian parents which causes them to have low spiritual expectations for their small children. From this mentality has come the concept of "children's church" in which children are separated from the main body of the church during worship. Likewise, little children are often left out of Bible study in the home because parents do not believe their children are ready to learn from God's word. When Christian parents underestimate their children's ability to benefit from God's word, they deprive the children of precious instruction during their most formative years.

To avoid this pitfall for your young children, you should understand that they have a tremendous capacity for learning even in their earliest years. As the saying goes, you must "strike while the iron is hot." Consider the example of Timothy, who was taught God's word by his mother and grandmother (2 Timothy 1:5). The apostle Paul wrote to him in 2 Timothy 3:14-15 (emphasis added):

> You, however, continue in the things you have learned and become convinced of, knowing from whom you have learned them, and that **from childhood you have known the sacred writings** which are able to give you the wisdom that leads to salvation through faith which is in Christ Jesus.

The word "childhood" in this passage comes from the Greek word *brephos*, which means a newborn child, an infant, or a babe. This means that Timothy had been taught God's word from infancy. This childhood training in the Scriptures continued to benefit Timothy throughout his adulthood, for it provided the wisdom to lead him to salvation and to equip him for every good work (2 Timothy 3:16-17). This is the most important fulfillment of Proverbs 22:6 – "Train up a child in the way he should go, even when he is old he will not depart from it." You can never start that kind of training too soon, for the Scripture says to God, "Out of the mouth of infants and nursing babies You have prepared praise for Yourself" (Matthew 21:16; ref. Psalm 8:2).

Of course, Bible lessons are not the only instructions that you will be teaching to your little children, but all of your lessons should be grounded in God's word and motivated by godliness. As I said in my previous letter[103], God's word is the basis for understanding everything in the world, and it must be the foundation for every-thing you teach to your children. Even when your infant or toddler cannot understand the godly motivation behind each lesson, your godly attitude and love for God will gradually be transferred to your child. "A pupil is not above his teacher; but everyone, after he has been fully trained, will be like his teacher" (Luke 6:40). Your godly attitude makes every lesson you teach honorable to God and sig-nificant to your child, whether you are teaching letters, numbers, colors, Bible stories, how to tie shoes, or anything else.

As you open your eyes to the need of early education for your little children, you should also realize that you are not the only one who wants to shape your children's minds while they are most im-pressionable. There are many forces competing for your children's hearts and souls. I told you in an earlier letter that the National Education Association (NEA) already recognizes the importance of your children's earliest years, and it has resolved to support "early childhood education programs" in the public schools beginning at birth.[104] The NEA also supports legislation that would require children to attend such programs from birth, which is a purely Marxist (communist) concept. I do not intend to imply in any way that the NEA fulfills any particular Bible prophecy, but the situation does remind me of the scene described in Revelation 12:4 – "And the dragon stood before the woman who was about to give birth, so that when she gave birth he might devour her child."

---

[103] See Chapter 17, "A Plan for Homeschooling."

[104] See Chapter 12, "Government Schools."

Actually, a government program for early childhood education already exists, although attendance in its schools is not mandatory. It is called Head Start, which is a federal program that started in 1965 and is presently funded by taxpayers at a rate of about $8 billion per year.[105] While Head Start is intended to assist low-income families with early education, it has been found to be ineffective in its purposes[106] and plagued with fraud.[107] It is no surprise that Head Start suffers from the same defects as public schools, for it really is just public school for little children. The concern about Head Start for you as a Christian parent is that the structure for compulsory early education is already in place. If the NEA gets its way and the United Nations' Convention of the Rights of the Child (CRC) becomes law in the United States, then it will be easy for the government to implement compulsory early education for all children. Let's pray that does not happen.

In these modern times, it has become common practice for most parents to send their children to some form of early education, whether it is Head Start, preschool, or just daycare. For many newborn children, they have no more than six weeks with their mothers before they are given to others for daily care and training. Don't let this trend influence you in any way. You are not trying to keep up with the world, but rather you are trying to keep away from the worldly influences that can harm your children. Your goal is simply to bring up your children in "the discipline and instruction of the Lord" (Ephesians 6:4).

By the way, I mentioned before that sometimes little children are described as "preschoolers," but let's reconsider that term for a moment. To call a child a "preschooler" implies that he is predestined for school, but this isn't true for a child who is to be homeschooled. A homeschooled child will not go to school at all, but instead he commences his education as soon as his parents impart the first lesson of life. This is another point where we ought to de-

---

[105] Budget for Head Start retrieved 6/20/11 from National Head Start Association website, www.nhsa.org.

[106] National 2010 Head Start Impact Study retrieved 6/20/11 from the Administration for Children & Families, U.S. Department of Health and Human Services website, www.acf.hhs.gov.

[107] John Diedrich and Amy Hetzner, "Fraud found at 2 Head Start centers in Wisconsin," Journal Sentinel, May 18, 2010. Retrieved 6/20/11 from www.jsonline.com.

part from worldly ways of thinking about education and embrace God's ways. Naturally, all infants begin to learn from their caregivers as soon as they are born, but the worldly concept of education requires for this first mode of learning to cease (or at least severely decrease) after a few years and for formal schooling to begin. In homeschool, the first mode of learning never ends until the child becomes an adult, which is as God would have it. Because this is true, a homeschooled child is never really a preschooler because he begins his education at birth and will not attend a formal school at all.

As you begin your own "head start" program of early education for your children, remember the plan for homeschooling that we derived from Deuteronomy 6:4-9.[108] This plan is summarized in four steps:

Step 1 – Parents must love God with all their heart, with all their soul, and with all their might.

Step 2 – Parents must have the word of God stamped on their hearts.

Step 3 – Parents must teach their children the word of God and a Biblical worldview.

Step 4 – Parents must teach their children with diligence, repetition, and constant exposure to the word of God.

There are no changes to this basic plan when very young children are taught. From age to age, the only differences are in the materials and approaches used to apply the plan. Obviously, older children can understand more than younger children, but this plan will govern the education of your children at all ages.

With this plan in mind, let's be more specific about how you can teach your little ones. Because God's word is the foundation of your teachings, you will certainly want to make a high priority of teaching the Bible to your young children. To that end, here are a few suggestions:

---

[108] See Chapter 17, "A Plan For Homeschooling."

- Don't be shy about reading directly from the Bible to your small children. They will understand more than you expect. After you read to them, do your best to explain the reading in a way that suits their level of ability (Nehemiah 8:8).
- You may choose to read from one of the many illustrated Bible story books that are written for small children – just be sure that the stories are truthful. Even babies can benefit from repeatedly hearing Bible stories and seeing the illustrations, for they will learn to recognize the stories, the characters, and the lessons. Always emphasize to your children that these stories are true and not like the stories they hear from fictitious books.
- As you go about your daily routine, talk about Bible truths with your children ("talk of them when you sit in your house and when you walk by the way and when you lie down and when you rise up"). Recognize opportunities that arise to illustrate Bible truths and make connections between your children's experiences and the words of the Bible.
- Teach your little ones the books of the Bible, the apostles, the tribes of Israel, the fruit of the spirit, etc. Lists like these are easy and fun for children to memorize, and they are essential to their Bible knowledge.
- You may even choose to have your children memorize Bible passages. Even before they can read, little children can be taught to recite the word of God. How precious is that!

You will also want to make worship an important part of your children's early education. Worship together with your children so that worship becomes an integral part of their lives. Pray together in the morning, before meals, at bedtime, and during the day – "pray without ceasing" (1 Thessalonians 5:17). Let them learn prayer as a habit that they will never forsake. Sing together with your children, for few things are as engaging to the mind and memory as music. Take advantage of the God-given blessing of your voices, and in this way you will "let the word of Christ richly dwell within you, with all wisdom teaching and admonishing one another with psalms and hymns and spiritual songs, singing with thankfulness in your hearts to God" (Colossians 3:16). Take your children into the assemblies of the church and let them participate in worship. Even if you spend an entire worship period struggling with your young child and trying to keep him quiet, it will be worth it for him to learn how to behave in the house of God.

Perhaps the best lessons that you can give to your little ones are those taught by your example. Let your young children see you working, serving, worshiping, and studying. Tell your children why you are doing these things, and explain your godly motivations. Be sure that your words are "good for edification according to the need of the moment, that it may give grace to those who hear" (Ephesians 4:29). Show them the virtues of godly relationships within the family, the church, and the community. Establish standards of godly behavior and good habits for your children, and lead them by example. Demonstrate to them your concern for others, and make them aware of your efforts to assist in others' needs. Teach them about authority by showing them your own obedience to God and requiring them to be obedient to you. In all things, let them learn to imitate you as you imitate Christ (1 Corinthians 11:1).

So where do math, science, history, English, and other school subjects fit into early education? If you follow the plan for homeschooling that we derived from Deuteronomy 6:4-9, then these subjects will fit in naturally and intrinsically. There will be plenty of opportunities for teaching your young children everything they need to know during their earliest years. Do not become overly concerned about a formal early education program or about pushing your small children to learn. God has equipped your little ones with more curiosity for learning that you will be able to satisfy. Of course, there are many materials and workbooks you can purchase to help teach your young children if you wish, but don't be stressed about it. Your best course will be to simply submit to the Lord, make His will your priority, stick to the plan, and take hold of the learning opportunities and teachable moments as they unfold. If you do these things, then your little ones will be well-prepared for the rest of their education and training.

I have more advice to help you get started in homeschooling, but I'll save it for future letters. For now, I hope that this letter has been enough to encourage you to begin teaching your little ones right away. Thank you for taking the time to read it. "May the LORD give you increase, you and your children" (Psalm 115:14).

Regards in the Lord,
Stacey

19

Teaching History

Dear Christian Parents,

As you take up the godly cause of educating your own children, I want you to focus on the importance of teaching one subject in particular. I believe that the way this subject has been taught (or mistaught) in the American public schools is a major factor in the current state of our nation. I also believe that if this subject is taught correctly to the current generation, then our children could see the dawn of a new era in which many of our modern problems would be solved. The subject of which I speak is history, and if you teach it well to your children, then it will be a great asset for cultivating faithfulness to God within them.

You have probably heard many times in recent years that America is lagging behind the rest of the world in the subjects of math and science. A resounding cry has risen up from the education professionals and politicians who demand improvements in math and science among American students. Organizations have been dedicated to raising awareness of our perceived math-and-science national crisis and to finding ways to close the competitive gap between America and the other nations of the world. There is one such organization whose motto is "Math + Science = Success," and their claim is, "Our nation's future just might depend on two simple words: math and science."[109] While I appreciate the value of math and science (I have a degree in engineering), and I know for certain that America is severely lacking in these subjects, I believe

---

[109] Retrieved 7/13/11 from Partnership for Reform in Science and Mathematics (PRISM) website, www.mathsciencesuccess.org.

that the hyper-emphasis now given to math and science is misplaced, for math and science alone can do nothing to solve our nation's most pressing problems.

Rather than tying our hopes for the nation's future to math and science education, the wiser approach is to give our children a solid foundation on meaningful history and then build the rest of their education in the light of that history. The reason I say this is because of the fundamental truth stated in **Proverbs 14:34 – "Righteousness exalts a nation, but sin is a disgrace to any people."** Likewise, **Psalm 33:12** declares, **"Blessed is the nation whose God is the LORD..."** Furthermore, **Psalm 9:17** says, **"The wicked will return to Sheol, even all the nations who forget God."** These passages show that a nation's success is not dependent upon things acquired through math and science, such as technological advances, new discoveries, new medicines, etc. Rather, a nation's success depends on its positive relationship with God, which is a fact taught with great clarity by history. A nation that learns the moral lessons of history will understand the key to godly success, and it will pursue the favor and blessings of God through righteousness. Math and science will find their rightful and fruitful places within a righteous nation, but without the guidance of history's hindsight, the subjects of math and science alone can never lead to the righteousness that "exalts a nation."

However, our nation is failing to teach meaningful history to our children. In 2010, the results from the National Assessment of Educational Progress (NAEP) showed that only 20 percent of fourth-graders and 17 percent of eighth-graders were proficient or advanced in their understanding of U.S. history. Worse still, only 12 percent of high school seniors were proficient.[110] Compare those results to NAEP's report for math in 2009, which showed that 39 percent of fourth-graders and 34 percent of eighth-graders were at or above proficient level.[111] If we have a crisis in math

---

[110] National Center for Education Statistics (2011). *The Nation's Report Card: U.S. History 2010* (NCES 2011–468). National Center for Education Statistics, Institute of Education Sciences, U.S. Department of Education, Washington, D.C. Retrieved 7/13/11 from nces.ed.gov.

[111] National Center for Education Statistics (2009). *The Nation's Report Card: Mathematics 2009* (NCES 2010–451). National Center for Education Statistics, Institute of Education Sciences, U.S. Department of Education, Washington, D.C. Retrieved 7/13/11 from nces.ed.gov.

education, then we have full catastrophe in history education. Yet these numbers only tell part of the story.

Notice that I said our children need a solid foundation on meaningful history. It is important to distinguish meaningful history from the meaningless history taught in the public schools, for meaningless history will never motivate students for righteousness. Students are often taught that history is nothing more than a series of disconnected events and a long, boring list of names, places, and dates to be memorized. They are not taught the spiritual lessons or the moral truths demonstrated by history because such teaching is not permitted in the government schools. When the study of history is robbed of its moral meaning by the schools, it becomes a pointless waste of time and effort. This is why I despised the subject of history when I was taught it in public schools. Now that I understand meaningful history, I find it to be fascinating. Maybe you also learned the meaningless public school version of history like I did, but now it is time for you to embrace meaningful history for the sake of yourself and your children.

So what is meaningful history? It is history that not only teaches names, events, dates, and places, but also discovers God's purposes and moral truths in the stories of the past. Meaningful history views past events in the context of a big picture so that history becomes one continuous story rather than a series of random, unrelated occurrences. When history is taught in a meaningful way, it becomes personal to the student, for he relates to the stories and sees how the past has affected his world today. He sees the present as the next chapter in the story of the world rather than an unrelated story of its own. Moreover, the student gains wisdom from the study of meaningful history, for the examples from the past give him an insightful way of evaluating the present and preparing for the future. He also learns a sense of gratitude for those who have sacrificed in earlier times to make his life better in the present. It was for this reason that John Adams appealed to us, saying:

Posterity: you will never know how much it has cost my generation to preserve your freedom. I hope you will make good use of it. If you do not, I shall repent in Heaven that I ever took half the pains to preserve it.[112]

Meaningful history demonstrates history's repetitious nature. In other words, it teaches students that current events and future events will always resemble past events. The wise man Solomon said it best when he wrote in Ecclesiastes 1:9 and 3:15:

> That which has been is that which will be, and that which has been done is that which will be done. So there is nothing new under the sun....That which is has been already and that which will be has already been, for God seeks what has passed by.

This means that a student of history can find answers to present and future problems by learning how similar problems were solved in the past. He can also avoid problems altogether by learning from the choices of others who came before him. This truth has been expressed by many wise men, such as the British statesman Edmund Burke, who has been attributed as saying, "Those who don't know history are destined to repeat it." A similar idea was expressed by Thomas Jefferson, who wrote:

> History by apprising them of the past will enable them to judge of the future; it will avail them of the experience of other times and other nations; it will qualify them as judges of the actions and designs of men; it will enable them to know ambition under every disguise it may assume; and knowing it, to defeat its views.[113]

Likewise, Patrick Henry said:

---

[112] From a letter to Abigail Adams, April 26, 1777; *Letters of John Adams, Addressed to His Wife. Edited by His Grandson, Charles Francis Adams*, Volume I (Boston: Charles C. Little and James Brown, 1841), p. 218. Retrieved 7/13/11 from books.google.com.

[113] Thomas Jefferson, *Notes on the State of Virginia* (London: John Stockdale, 1787), p. 248. Retrieved 7/13/11 from books.google.com.

I have but one lamp by which my feet are guided, and that is the lamp of experience. I know no way of judging of the future but by the past.[114]

Because these things are true, history is a valuable tool, for it allows a student to gain the wisdom of others' experiences without having to suffer their hardships. Give this tool to your children, and you will bless them.

Such meaningful history and its moral lessons can be taught through only one perspective, and that is the perspective given by the Bible. This is because the Biblical view of history is the only one that gives true purpose and context. It is also the only viewpoint that steers individuals and nations toward righteousness through which they may be exalted by God. Other viewpoints of history – naturalism, pantheism, modernism, postmodernism, etc. – demonstrate no purpose and give wholly unsatisfying explanations of the past. Only the Bible can give us a context for history that makes good sense.

The most important element of the Bible's context for understanding history is established in the very first verse of the Bible – "In the beginning God created the heavens and the earth" (Genesis 1:1). That foundational principle gives meaning to everything that follows, for the Creator of the world is also the Orchestrator of world history. Notice the words of God recorded in Isaiah 46:9-11:

Remember the former things long past, for I am God, and there is no other; I am God, and there is no one like Me, declaring the end from the beginning, and from ancient times things which have not been done, saying, "My purpose will be established, and I will accomplish all My good pleasure"...Truly I have spoken; truly I will bring it to pass. I have planned it, surely I will do it.

These words were spoken with reference to the destruction of Babylon, but they are true for every purpose of God throughout history. The Creator is **sovereign** (has the right and power to rule)

---

[114] Patrick Henry, Speech at the Second Virginia Convention at St. John's Church, Redmond, Virginia, March 23, 1775. Retrieved 7/13/11 from www.history.org.

over His creation and intervenes by His **providence** (foreseeing care and guidance) to achieve His purposes. I recommend that you read Psalm 33 as an exposition on the sovereignty of God and His involvement in the affairs of men. This psalm shows that God is involved in all history, which is a principle that was correctly stated by the great statesman Daniel Webster when he said, "History is God's providence in human affairs."[115]

With God as the central figure in all of history, the overall context of history given by the Bible can be summarized very simply. There are different ways to express this summary, but I will suggest six categories: **Creation, Sin, Flood, Babel, Christ, and Patience**.

- **Creation** – This category gives a context for explaining our origins and orders (Genesis 1:26-28) and for showing that everything God created in the beginning was very good (Genesis 1:31). This foundation of history is important to our understanding because it proves that our loving Creator did not make a world filled with death, suffering, disease, and destruction as we see today.

- **Sin** – The world was corrupted when Adam and Eve first committed sin, for death and all of its physical causes (suffering, disease, injury, etc.) affected the earth (Genesis 2:15-17; 3:1-24; Romans 6:23a; 8:20-22). Because of sin, the original, "very good" creation of God was corrupted, and this gives a context for understanding all of the suffering and death in the world today.

- **Flood** – The global flood was brought upon the world during Noah's time because "the wickedness of man was great on the earth" (Genesis 6:5). This gives us a context for understanding certain elements of natural history that were caused by this global catastrophe, such as fossils, geological features, and the earth's present volatile climate.

- **Babel** – The events at Babel resulted in the scattering of people over the face of the earth (Genesis 11:1-9). This history gives us a context for understanding the origin of languages, cultures, and nations.

---

[115]Daniel Webster, *The Works of Daniel Webster* (Boston: Charles C. Little and James Brown, 1851), p. 399. Retrieved 7/13/11 from books.google.com.

- **Christ** – Christ came into the world to become the Redeemer of mankind, and He accomplished this purpose by means of His death on the cross and His resurrection. These facts give us a context for understanding God's works during Old Testament times from Abraham until Christ came, for He was unfolding His plan through Abraham to bring the Savior into the world (Mark 1:15; Galatians 4:4-5; Ephesians 2:11-22). They also give us a context for understanding the New Testament era and the beginning of the church.
- **Patience** – This category gives us a context for understanding the time in which we now live and the final events of history. This present period of history is defined by God's patience as He wishes for all to come to repentance, and it will end when the Lord returns and the world is destroyed by fire (2 Peter 3:3-13). This period is also marked by our patience as we wait for the return of Christ from heaven (1 Thessalonians 1:10; 5:1-11; James 5:7-8).

Taken altogether, this Biblical summary gives us a solid foundation and a big-picture context for making sense of history.

Without the context of a Biblical viewpoint that sees the hand of God in world events, history becomes confusing. If history is taught without telling of God's providence or His immutable laws, then it is a rambling story without a moral and an incoherent message without meaning. The need for teaching history in a meaningful way is perfectly expressed in the following words from the introduction to the 1878 history textbook *The Story of Liberty*:

There is still one other point: you will notice that while the oppressors have carried out their plans, and had things their own way, there were other forces silently at work, which in time undermined their plans, as if a Divine hand were directing the counter-plan. Whoever peruses the "Story of Liberty" without recognizing this feature will fail of fully comprehending the meaning of history. There must be a meaning to history, or else existence is an incomprehensible enigma.[116]

---

116 Charles Carleton Coffin, *The Story of Liberty* (New York: Harper and Brothers, 1878) p. 9. Retrieved 7/13/11 from books.google.com.

Indeed, only a Biblical foundation with God as the cornerstone can provide the basis for putting the pieces of history's puzzle together.

Before going any farther, I need to offer a word of caution to you about teaching history with a Biblical viewpoint. Although we know that God is sovereign and works providentially in the affairs of men, we must not assume anything about God's purposes or involvement in world events. Instead, we must abide strictly by what is written in God's word. In the case of an event that is recorded in the Bible, we may safely teach God's specific purposes and actions because they have been revealed by the Holy Spirit through the Scriptures. (For example, consider the first destruction of Jerusalem, which is explained in 2 Chronicles 36:13-21.) However, in the case of a historical event that is not recorded in the Bible, we cannot be as assertive. In that case, we must stick to what we know, such as whether the people and nations involved in the event honored or violated God's laws or how the outcome of the event harmonizes with principles of God's word. By teaching history in this way, we can still demonstrate God's sovereignty and providence in the world even when we do not know exactly how God has intervened in specific events.

I give you this warning because there is a common belief among professing Christians that every occurrence in the world happens by the will of God, and that simply is not true. Those who hold this belief will even attribute evil to the will of God, and that is wrong (James 1:13-18). God has allowed man to have free will (Joshua 24:15), and with that free will comes the ability to defy God's will and commit sin. Sin is transgression of God's will, and every time sin is committed in the world, God's will has been violated. Likewise, the effects and consequences of sin are not according to God's desires, for the Lord is "not wishing for any to perish but for all to come to repentance" (2 Peter 3:9; see also Matthew 18:14). God "desires all men to be saved and to come to the knowledge of the truth" (1 Timothy 2:4), but not all will be saved (Matthew 7:13-14, 21-23; 22:14; Luke 13:23-30). Sin and its consequences occur as the result of the activity of Satan, which God permits and limits but does not cause or desire (Job 1:1-2:10; 42:10-17). Therefore, it is an error to say that everything happens according to God's will, for if God's will was always done on earth, then it would not be necessary for us to pray, "Thy will be done on earth as it is in heaven" (Matthew 6:10).

This false belief concerning God's will is the product of a misunderstanding about the sovereignty of God. The fact that God is sovereign means that He has the right and power to rule over the world, but some misunderstand this to mean He controls every word, deed, and thought of every person. Likewise, the Bible says that "God causes all things to work together for good to those who love God" (Romans 8:28), but some misunderstand this to mean "all things" are somehow good or that every event must be a result of God's will. The Bible even shows that God uses evil persons (such as the betrayer Judas) and nations (such as Assyria) to accomplish His purposes, but this does not mean that He causes them to do evil or that it is His will for them to sin. Instead of these misconceptions about God's sovereignty, the Bible teaches that the sovereign will of God ultimately will be fulfilled when the Lord Christ returns to reward the faithful and execute judgment on those who have rejected Him (Romans 2:5-10; 2 Corinthians 5:10; 2 Thessalonians 1:5-10; 2 Peter 3:3-13). Until then, violations of the will of God will continue to happen, but they are not violations of God's sovereignty.

Now that you have established a Biblical context with a correct foundation on God's sovereignty and providence, you are ready to teach meaningful history to your children. When you do, you will be carrying on the ancient tradition and responsibility of all godly parents, who are to teach their children about the events that preceded them so that they will gain an appreciation for the world they have entered.

This is the reason Israel was commanded to teach history to their children, for an understanding of their history would allow their lives to "go well" in their land (Deuteronomy 4:9, 40; Psalm 78:1-8). The parents of Israel were also told to use the history of their people as the means to teach their children the meaning of God's testimonies, statutes, and judgments (Deuteronomy 6:20-25). Furthermore, Israel was required to establish certain memorials of their history as a way to provoke their children's curiosity about what God had done for their people (Exodus 12:14; Joshua 24:1-11, 20-24). We now need to carry on this tradition by teaching history to our children so that they will appreciate what God has done for His people in Christ, for America, and for the world.

Finally, I will leave you with a few words of Scripture to drive home the point and emphasize the value of historical knowledge.

Remember the days of old, consider the years of all generations. Ask your father, and he will inform you, your elders, and they will tell you. (Deuteronomy 32:7)

Please inquire of past generations, and consider the things searched out by their fathers. For we are only of yesterday and know nothing, because our days on earth are as a shadow. Will they not teach you and tell you, and bring forth words from their minds? (Job 8:8-10)

I have considered the days of old, the years of long ago. (Psalm 77:5)

I remember the days of old; I meditate on all Your doings; I muse on the work of Your hands. (Psalm 143:5)

Thus says the LORD, "Stand by the ways and see and ask for the ancient paths, where the good way is, and walk in it; and you will find rest for your souls…" (Jeremiah 6:16)

For whatever was written in earlier times was written for our instruction, so that through perseverance and the encouragement of the Scriptures we might have hope. (Romans 15:4)

Now these things happened as examples for us, so that we would not crave evil things as they also craved…Now these things happened to them as an example, and they were written for our instruction, upon whom the ends of the ages have come. (1 Corinthians 10:6, 11)

I do not mean to overplay the importance of teaching history, but as you can see, it truly is imperative. I assure you that the opponents of God know that the teaching of history is essential to their success or failure. They abide by this slogan from George Orwell's *Nineteen Eighty-Four*: "Who controls the past controls the future: who controls the present controls the past."[117]   This is the reason they have rewritten history and worked to take away its moral meaning in the public schools, for by doing so they have guaranteed that generations of students will walk in darkness. Don't let your children be among those students.   Teach them in the light of meaningful, God-centered history, and they will learn to trust in God.

Regards in the Lord,
Stacey

---

[117] George Orwell, *Nineteen Eighty-Four* (New York: Harcourt, Brace & Co., 1949), p. 309. Retrieved 7/13/11 from books.google.com.

20

A Letter to Fathers

Dear Christian Fathers,

"I am writing to you, fathers, because you know Him who has been from the beginning" (1 John 2:13-14). These words from the aged apostle John were addressed to the elder men in the church whom he designated as "fathers" in contrast to the young men whom he also addressed. These fathers were mature men in the faith who knew "Him who has been from the beginning," i.e., Jesus Christ, the Word who was in the beginning with God and who was God (John 1:1-3). Because of their knowledge of the eternal Son of God and their spiritual relationship with Him, these fathers were true leaders in the church. John appealed to them because their leadership was crucial in guiding the church in faith and love and in protecting the church from worldly influences.

I am invoking the inspired words of the apostle John because I have some important words to say to you Christian fathers about your role in homeschooling. In fact, much of what I have to say pertains to fatherhood and the home in general, but it is especially important for you now as you take on the task of educating your children. Each of you is the designated leader of your home, and your active leadership, support, and participation in your home-school is essential for success. Your knowledge of the Lord and your relationship with Him should cause you to understand the crucial part you have in the education God has ordained for your children.

Let's begin by considering the Biblical model of a father. According to the Bible, fatherhood requires much more than a mere biological relationship. In the original language of the New Testament, the word for father is *pater* (the root of the English word "paternity"), and it means "a nourisher, protector, and upholder." The typical use of this word in the Bible is for a biological ancestor, but the original definition of *pater* says nothing of a biological relationship. Instead, *pater* describes the nature of a man's relationship and responsibility toward a child. Therefore, the qualification for fatherhood is not simply the ability to conceive a child. **A man who would be a father must be willing and able to take on the roles of nourisher, protector, and upholder.** This means that a man must provide a home in which a child will be nourished, protected, and upheld in order for him to be a father. A man does not simply become a father, but rather he makes himself to be a father by his actions toward his child.

A true father is a man who takes responsibility for raising a child. A biological father naturally has this responsibility for his offspring, for God requires him to care for his own family (1 Timothy 5:8). Some men assume the role of fathers for children who are not their own, and their fatherhood is not diminished due to the lack of biological relationships. Consider the example of Joseph, who was a father to Jesus in every way even though Joseph did not conceive Jesus (Matthew 13:55; Mark 6:3; Luke 2:33, 39-52; John 6:42). Also consider Job, who said, "I became a father to the needy" (Job 29:16; see also 31:16-23), indicating his father-like provision of nourishment and protection for those in need. Many men have provided homes for orphaned children and have thus made themselves fathers, such as Job did. (Notice that the word "orphan," which comes from the Greek word *orphanos*, means "fatherless." In the O.T., both children without parents and children of widows were considered orphans.)

By definition, a family is to be characterized by a father. The word most often translated as "family" in the New Testament is the Greek word *patria*, which is derived from *pater*, the word we noticed before for "father." Consider Ephesians 3:14-15 — "For this reason, I bow my knees before the Father, from whom every family in heaven and on earth derives its name..." Notice the play on the words "Father" (*pater*), in reference to God, and "family" (*patria*) in this passage. The similarity of these words indicates the intimacy and integrity of the relationship of a father to his family. Therefore, **a family is to be an extension of a father.** This is true for the whole family, including the children and their mother. They are all under his care and authority. Although every family does not fit this mold, God's original, ideal design for the family would have the family to derive its character from a godly father and even more so from the Father in heaven.

Just as I have encouraged you throughout these letters to conform to the Biblical model of education for your children, I now encourage you fathers to conform to the Biblical model of fatherhood. As a husband and father, you are the nourisher, protector, and upholder for your family. If you do not fulfill your proper role, then your family's homeschool will fall short of what it could be. In fact, it is likely to fail altogether, for a home cannot achieve its goal without the consent and support of its leader. As the person who will characterize your family, you have many responsibilities to tend.

One responsibility you have as a father is to be a godly leader in your home. As the God-delegated head of your home, you have the natural burden of leadership for your family. You must lead your home foremost by your own exemplary words and deeds. As I said in an earlier letter, the best lessons that you can give to your little ones are those taught by your example. Your righteous example will be a blessing to your children, for Proverbs 20:7 says, "A righteous man who walks in his integrity – how blessed are his sons after him." As a leader, you must also establish the godly goals for your home and see to it that they are achieved by all who are under your authority. If there is anything in your home or anywhere else that hinders your children from accomplishing your godly goals, then eliminate those obstacles from your children's path. In this way, you fulfill your role as **protector of your children.**

Another responsibility for you as a father is to be a godly teacher and trainer of your children in your home. You need to be active in the oversight and instruction of your family's homeschool. Ephesians 6:4 says, "And, fathers, do not provoke your children to anger; but bring them up in the discipline and instruction of the Lord." Notice that this responsibility is explicitly assigned to fathers rather than the common, modern practice of assigning the responsibility to mothers. The phrase "bring them up" in the NASB translation means to "nourish them." In other words, you are to feed your children's souls on the discipline and instruction of the Lord. "Discipline" indicates that you are to give physical direction or correction to your children, and "instruction" indicates that you are to give them verbal direction. These two methods will give your children the complete spiritual nourishment they need and allow you to fulfill your role as **nourisher of your children.**

Let's give a little more thought to the subject of your children's discipline for a moment. The responsibility of discipline can be difficult and burdensome, but your loving discipline is absolutely necessary for the education and training of your children. A loving father will discipline his child because he realizes the child needs it (Proverbs 3:12; 13:24; 19:18; 22:15; 23:13-14; 29:15, 17). Without discipline from a father, it is as if a child has no father at all, for undisciplined, unloved children are as "illegitimate children and not sons" (Hebrews 12:8). If you would not want your children to be orphaned, then don't leave them undisciplined.

Therefore, perform your duty as a father and discipline your children, yet do so in a compassionate way that demonstrates your fatherly love (Psa. 103:13). Again, notice Ephesians 6:4, which says, "Fathers, do not provoke your children to anger," and also consider the sister verse of Colossians 3:21, which says, "Fathers, do not exasperate your children, so that they will not lose heart." You must exercise discipline, but don't do it in such a heavy-handed way that you frustrate your children or crush their spirits. Of course, your children will never enjoy the discipline you give, for "all discipline for the moment seems not to be joyful, but sorrowful" (Hebrews 12:11a). Nevertheless, they will respect you for lovingly disciplining them for their own good (Hebrews 12:9), and the result will be that they will yield "the peaceful fruit of righteousness" (Hebrews 12:11b), which is your goal for your children. In the end, you will always be glad that you disciplined your children in the right way, for as Proverbs 29:17 says, "Correct your son, and he will give you comfort; he will also delight your soul."

Another responsibility for you as a father is to be the provider for your home. Not only are you to provide spiritual nourishment to your children through the discipline and instruction of the Lord, but you are also to provide for their physical needs (food, clothing, shelter, safety, protection, etc.). 1 Timothy 5:8 says, "But if anyone does not provide for his own, and especially for those of his household, he has denied the faith and is worse than an unbeliever." This passage along with others (Proverbs 6:6-11; 24:30-34; 2 Thessalonians 3:6-15) shows the depth of God's contempt for those who will not work and provide for their own. This fundamental premise of God's word is too often forgotten by worthless men who abandon their children to mothers without support.

Of course, you are already providing for your family's physical needs, but you will have to do even more in order to homeschool. Specifically, you must do whatever is necessary within godly means to allow your wife to stay at home with your children rather than having to leave them and go to a job. She cannot be a worker at home (Titus 2:5) if you require her to go out of the home for work. It is not impossible for two parents working fulltime outside the home to homeschool, but it is very difficult and extremely rare. Therefore, it is up to you to provide the income, set the family budget, avoid and eliminate debt, and do anything else necessary to provide for your family's needs physically, spiritually, educationally, and otherwise. In this way, you fulfill your fatherly role as **upholder of your children.**

Your performance of these responsibilities is crucial to your children both physically and spiritually. Naturally, you realize that your children need physical sustenance to live and grow as they should. However, your children's spiritual needs are even more important, and you are the key figure for their spiritual growth. You must realize that **the relationship between a father and his child is a model for the child of the child's future relationship with God.** By representing authority and providence, the father represents to his young child a figure of God Himself, our heavenly Father. The figure of fatherhood is used repeatedly in Scripture to describe God, so your representation of that figure has a profound effect upon your children's understanding of God. That is how important you are to your children's godly education!

As if that is not enough to convince you of the importance of your role in your family's homeschool, there is another compelling reason. Over and over again, the Bible demonstrates that a father is vital not only in the teaching of his children, but also in the destiny of his future descendants. For example, consider the first five verses of Proverbs 4:

Hear, O sons, the instruction of a father, and give attention that you may gain understanding, for I give you sound teaching; do not abandon my instruction. When I was a son to my father, tender and the only son in the sight of my mother, then he taught me and said to me, "Let your heart hold fast my words;

keep my commandments and live; acquire wisdom! Acquire understanding! Do not forget nor turn away from the words of my mouth."

Notice how this wisdom is to be passed from generation to generation, from father to son to grandson. In God's design, each generation of a family is to be built upon previous generations, for "grandchildren are the crown of old men, and the glory of sons is their fathers" (Proverbs 17:6). God's word says, "In place of your fathers will be your sons; you shall make them princes in all the earth" (Psalm 45:16).

I don't mean to overwhelm you, but your responsibility as a father is not only to teach your children, but it is also to teach your children to teach their children. **"Tell your sons about it, and let your sons tell their sons, and their sons the next generation" (Joel 1:3).** God has always expected fathers to teach their children in this way, for He even commanded Israel, "Only give heed to yourself and keep your soul diligently, so that you do not forget the things which your eyes have seen and they do not depart from your heart all the days of your life; but make them known to your sons and your grandsons" (Deuteronomy 4:9). Consider also Deuteronomy 32:7, which says, "Remember the days of old, consider the years of all generations. Ask your father, and he will inform you, your elders, and they will tell you." As our children look for answers from generations past, it is our obligation to give them those answers for their sake and for the sake of generations yet to come. In this way, we fathers have a responsibility for the fate of our future descendants. Think about that!

The generational responsibility of a father is clearly expressed in Psalm 78:2-8. Notice these verses, and give particular attention to verse 5:

²I will open my mouth in a parable; I will utter dark sayings of old,
³Which we have heard and known, and our fathers have told us.
⁴We will not conceal them from their children, but tell to the generation to come the praises of the LORD, and His strength and His wondrous works that He has done.

⁵For He established a testimony in Jacob and appointed a law in Israel, which He commanded our fathers that they should teach them to their children,
⁶That the generation to come might know, even the children yet to be born, that they may arise and tell them to their children,
⁷That they should put their confidence in God and not forget the works of God, but keep His commandments,
⁸And not be like their fathers, a stubborn and rebellious generation, a generation that did not prepare its heart and whose spirit was not faithful to God.

I realize that the term "fathers" in this passage and many others is used in the sense of forefathers or ancestors of the nation of Israel, but nonetheless these passages contain a vital lesson for every individual father. Given all that the Bible teaches about the responsibility of a father to teach his children, I have no doubt that these passages can be applied to every individual father and his particular family.

The willingness and ability to carry the responsibility of fatherhood to generations was the reason that God chose Abraham to be the father of His people. His names – Abram, meaning "exalted father," and Abraham, meaning "father of a multitude" – were significant of this godly trait of generational fatherhood. Notice God's testimony of Abraham's fatherhood in Genesis 18:19 – "For I have chosen him, so that he may command his children and his household after him to keep the way of the LORD by doing righteousness and justice, so that the LORD may bring upon Abraham what He has spoken about him." Indeed, Abraham did command his children, and his physical descendants became the nation of Israel (and several other nations as well), while his spiritual descendants by faith are today's Christians (Galatians 3:7, 29).

Another example of how one father can profoundly affect many generations of his descendants is that of Jonadab. This rather obscure character from the Old Testament is first mentioned as Jehonadab the son of Rechab in 2 Kings 10:15-28. This was an occasion when Israel's King Jehu was destroying the house of Ahab and the worshipers of Baal. After Jehu confirmed that Jehonadab's heart was right (v. 15), he brought him along on his God-given mission. The next time Jonadab is mentioned is in Jeremiah 35 during the reign of Jehoiakim in Judah more than 200 years later. In this chapter, God used the descendants of Jonadab as an example to teach Judah about faithful children who obeyed their father. Notice the words of Jonadab's descendants in Jeremiah 35:6-10:

> We will not drink wine, for Jonadab the son of Rechab, our father, commanded us, saying, "You shall not drink wine, you or your sons, forever. You shall not build a house, and you shall not sow seed and you shall not plant a vineyard or own one; but in tents you shall dwell all your days, that you may live many days in the land where you sojourn." We have obeyed the voice of Jonadab the son of Rechab, our father, in all that he commanded us, not to drink wine all our days, we, our wives, our sons or our daughters, nor to build ourselves houses to dwell in; and we do not have vineyard or field or seed. We have only dwelt in tents, and have obeyed and have done according to all that Jonadab our father commanded us.

After perhaps eight generations of descendants, the faithful leadership of Jonadab had been effective in preserving his family through the destruction of one nation (the northern kingdom of Israel) and was still effective in the midst of Judah's national destruction. Because of this, God said, "Jonadab the son of Rechab shall not lack a man to stand before Me always" (v. 19).

Can we Christian fathers have such a profound effect upon generations of our descendants? We may not live to see the outcome of our family trees, but our responsibility before God to our descendants begins today. "A good man leaves an inheritance to his children's children" (Proverbs 13:22), and our inheritance to our children's children must be our faith. Our faith is in the God who says, "Train up a child in the way he should go, even when he is old he will not depart from it" (Proverbs 22:6). In order for our children to follow "the way [they] should go," we must be fully involved in every aspect of their upbringing. I am fully convinced that homeschooling is the best way to fulfill this fatherly responsibility in the area of education, and I hope that you are, too.

Before I close this letter, there is one more minor issue that I must address that often becomes an obstacle to fathers in homeschooling. That issue is sports. Many men will dismiss homeschooling because they want their children to be involved in school sports teams. If this is an obstacle for you, then let me help you to set it aside. There are enough homeschooling groups now forming sports teams that you can probably find a place for your children to play just about any sport you want.

However, the issue of sports is not really about sports. If your concern over sports, band, or any other extracurricular activity prevents you from educating your children in the best way to cultivate faithfulness to God in them, then your priorities are very, very wrong. In this case, you need to go back to our plan for homeschooling[118] and start over with Step 1 – Parents must love God with all their heart, with all their soul, and with all their might. I also offer you a warning about public schools that permit homeschool students to play on their sports teams. Many such schools offer these opportunities as a way of drawing homeschoolers into their control. Don't be fooled by this tactic. Moreover, if you are trying to avoid the bad socialization of public schools, then you need to avoid them altogether, including their sports.

In a time when fathers are often absent from the home, and those who are present are often failing to carry out their responsibilities, your godly work of fatherhood is desperately needed in your home. It is time "to turn the hearts of the fathers back to the children, and the disobedient to the attitude of the righteous, so as to make ready a people prepared for the Lord" (Luke 1:17). Don't forget the things I have said to you in this letter, and lead your family in education and in every other part of life. Your children are depending on you in every sense of the word.

I would be remiss if I didn't mention that one of the best things you can do for your children is to be a godly husband to their mother. In my next letter, I will address the role of Christian mothers in a godly home and homeschool. Your own godly wife is a precious partner with you in this venture of homeschooling, "for her worth is far above jewels" (Proverbs 31:10). Together with the help of the Lord, you can raise up godly children unto God's honor and glory.

Regards in the Lord,
Stacey

---

[118] See Chapter 17, "A Plan for Homeschooling."

21

A Letter to Mothers

Dear Christian Mothers,

"My mother was always on the run – always the last to start her dinner and the first to finish. For, if my father was the head of our house, my mother was its heart." This is a line from one of my favorite old movies,[119] and it perfectly captures the image of a godly mother in her home. This image is magnified in families that homeschool, for while fathers are vitally important in homeschooling,[120] most homeschooling would never happen without mothers. This is by God's design, for He intended for a wife and mother to be a worker in her home, and the education of her children is a core part of her work.

The work of a mother in a home and in a homeschool is not easy, and it is not to be taken lightly. Motherhood is a high and noble calling that is precious in the sight of God and eternally important for children. When you were blessed to become a mother, you were made a steward of God's gift and heritage, for "the fruit of the womb is a reward" (Psalm 127:3). For this reason, I write this letter to encourage you mothers to fully embrace the challenge of homeschooling as a good steward of God's precious gift so that you may experience all the joy of godly motherhood as your children learn from you how to walk in truth (2 John 4; 3 John 4).

There is no doubt that a mother has a profound effect on the life of her children. In fact, the influence of mothers is so profound

---

[119] *How Green Was My Valley*, 1940.

[120] See Chapter 20, "A Letter to Fathers."

that it has changed the courses of nations and the world. In 1865, William Ross Wallace wrote the poem *The Hand That Rocks the Cradle is the Hand that Rules the World*, and history demonstrates that his words are true. Consider a few quotes from some former United States presidents about their mothers:

"All that I am my mother made me." – JOHN QUINCY ADAMS[121]

"The memory of my mother and her teachings were the only capital I had to start life with, and on that capital I have made my way." – ANDREW JACKSON[122]

"All that I am, and all that I hope to be, I owe to my angel mother." – ABRAHAM LINCOLN[123]

We can look on these men as positive examples of mothers' influence for which we should all be thankful.

There are also negative examples of a mother's influence, such as that of Jezebel. She incited her husband, King Ahab of Israel, to reject God and worship Baal (1 Kings 21:25), and their sons (Ahaziah and Joram in Israel) and grandson (Ahaziah in Judah) became exceedingly wicked kings. Likewise, Jezebel's daughter, Athaliah, made herself queen over Judah and even murdered her own grandchildren to protect her throne (2 Kings 11:1-3). These examples prove that the influence of mothers on their children matters more than we can begin to measure.

Therefore, every mother should seek to have the very best influence possible on her children. Of course, there is no better influence on children than that which cultivates faithfulness to God within them, which is the main goal accomplished by Christian homeschooling. As you have seen in this series of letters, the goal

---

[121] ,*The Expositor and Current Anecdotes*, Vol. 13 (Cleveland, Ohio: F.M. Barton, 1911), p. 506. Retrieved 7/13/11 from books.google.com.

[122] Augustus C. Buell, *History of Andrew Jackson: Pioneer, Patriot, Soldier, Politician, President*, Vol. 1 (New York: Charles Scribner's Sons, 1904), p. 57. Retrieved 7/13/11 from books.google.com.

[123] James Baldwin, *Abraham Lincoln: A True Life* (New York: American Book Co., 1904), p. 54. Retrieved 7/13/11 from books.google.com.

of faithfulness cannot be achieved through the modern model of surrendering children to public schools for their education. Children desperately need their mothers to be with them and to teach them, but too many mothers are turning their children over to substitutes for these needs while they pursue other goals. Those mothers who choose to stay at home and teach their own children are rejecting the pressures of the world in favor of God's design, and their children are reaping the benefits of God's wisdom and the faithfulness of this godly choice.

As you now seek to have the best influence on your own children through homeschooling, your faith in God must be stronger than ever. **You must believe that God's design for motherhood is divinely powerful for bringing up children.** To make this point, consider for a moment God's wondrous design for the natural, physical process of conception, development, and birth of children that occurs through mothers. David marveled at these thoughts when he wrote Psalm 139:13-16:

> For You formed my inward parts; You wove me in my mother's womb. I will give thanks to You, for I am fearfully and wonderfully made; wonderful are Your works, and my soul knows it very well. My frame was not hidden from You, when I was made in secret, and skillfully wrought in the depths of the earth; Your eyes have seen my unformed substance; and in Your book were all written the days that were ordained for me, when as yet there was not one of them.

Certainly, we are amazed by the wisdom of God in this physical process, but let us recognize that the same wise God who designed the physical process has also ordained the spiritual process for bringing up children in their mothers' care. We know that God's design of the womb is powerful for the development of children's bodies, so why would we not trust that His design for motherhood is equally powerful for the development of children's minds and souls? For this reason, I urge you mothers to trust the Biblical model of motherhood just as I have encouraged you throughout these letters to trust the Biblical model for the education for your children.

In God's design of motherhood, He has blessed mothers and equipped them with a natural affection for their own sons and daughters. Some have called this natural affection a maternal instinct, and Scripture often makes reference to this natural bond between mother and child. For example, God's word presents a mother's love and compassion as an enduring bond that does not break, asking, "Can a woman forget her nursing child, and have no compassion on the son of her womb?" (Isaiah 49:15). Scripture also uses a mother's love as the model of comfort, for Isaiah 66:13 says, "As one whom his mother comforts, so I will comfort you." When Paul described his care for the church at Thessalonica, he used the figure of a mother, saying, "But we proved to be gentle among you, as a nursing mother tenderly cares for her own children" (1 Thessalonians 2:7). By these passages of God's word, we see that the maternal instinct has become the gold standard of love, compassion, comfort, and care.

This natural, maternal affection manifests itself through a mother's tireless efforts to do the best for her children. These efforts begin immediately, for as soon as a child is born, a woman forgets the pain of birth and embraces the joyful work of motherhood (John 16:21). Consider some examples from Scripture of mothers acting on their natural affection for their children:

- Jochebed's love for her son Moses moved her to save him when Pharaoh commanded for all the newborn sons of Israel to be killed (Exodus 1:22-2:10).

- Hannah dedicated her son Samuel to God and gave him to serve the Lord before Eli the priest (1 Samuel 1:11, 19-2:11). Her continued love and care for her son was evident when she made him a new robe every year (1 Samuel 2:19), and she was blessed by her son becoming one of the greatest men in Israel's history, serving as a prophet, priest, and judge of God's people. By the way, notice that even though Samuel was dedicated for such important work, his mother would not release him from her care until he was weaned, which was likely no earlier than two years of age. Compare that to today's children whose mothers often surrender them to others when they are six weeks old.

- Solomon provoked the natural, maternal affection to identify a mother when two women disputed a claim to the same child (1 Kings 3:16-27). The woman who preferred to give up the child rather than have him killed revealed her maternal love, and Solomon gave her the child.

- A faithful Canaanite woman's love of her daughter moved her to plead with the Lord for her daughter's healing, which the Lord granted (Matthew 15:21-28).

These examples are typical of mothers who work and pray for their children, instilling in their children a sense of love and security that comforts them for their entire lives. Many have noted that on fields of battle, in every culture, era, and language, a soldier's dying words are most often to cry for his mother in a desperate plea for comfort. Consider that one of the few comforts our Lord received as He died on the cross was that His mother was there (John 19:25). How anguished Mary's life must have been, knowing Jesus as she did (Luke 2:19, 34-35, 51), and yet she was at His side until the end.

The maternal instinct of natural, godly affection for your children will serve you well as you educate them. Your innate desire to see your children grow, learn, and flourish will motivate you when nothing else will. There will likely be times when frustration, exhaustion, burnout, and weariness will sap your enthusiasm and energy for homeschooling, but your maternal drive will push you on. God gave you that impulse for your children's benefit, and no one else has such a desire for them but you.

Sadly, many pressures in our society influence women to suppress their natural affection for their children. They have been convinced that the home is too small of a place for them and that motherhood is not a sufficient use of their time. To be a "stay-at-home mom" is considered degrading and out-dated by feminists, and the idea of homeschooling is utterly rejected. Instead of conforming to the Biblical model of motherhood, American culture now encourages a modern woman to seek worldly success for her own sake. Moreover, the pressure for wealth and possessions has sent many mothers out of the home and away from their children. Certainly, some mothers have to work out of genuine necessity, and even the "excellent wife" of Proverbs 31 worked to support her home (Proverbs 31:16, 24). However, many mothers are compelled to work not by necessity but by the social and material expectations for a modern, two-income family or the need for perceived intellectual or emotional fulfillment. The end result is that the home and the children suffer because a mother is distracted from her God-given work in the home.

In God's design as revealed in the Biblical model, motherhood is primarily defined not by the maternal instinct but by the work a mother does. Among the various directions given to young women, Paul wrote for them to "love their children" (Titus 2:4-5). Notice that this love of children is not the natural affection that a mother feels for her children, but rather it is something that she must learn to do for her children. Older women are to train the younger women in this love of children, so it is truly an acquired skill. This same passage from Titus also commands women to be "workers at home" with the added motivation "that the word of God may not be dishonored." Similarly, Paul wrote to Timothy, "I want younger widows to get married, bear children, keep house, and give the enemy no occasion for reproach" (1 Timothy 5:14). These messages develop the image of a godly woman who is to be busy with her children in and about her home. This image is further revealed in the description of the excellent wife from Proverbs 31:10-31. Verse 27 of that passage says that such a woman "looks well to the ways of her household, and does not eat the bread of idleness." This is God's model of a true "working mother," and it is rightly characterized by the old saying, "A mother's work is never done."

A major part of the God-given work for a mother in her home is the teaching of her children. In my last letter,[124] I emphasized that Ephesians 6:4 gives the burden of bringing up children in "the discipline and instruction of the Lord" to fathers. However, mothers also have a significant responsibility in their children's teaching, including both discipline and instruction ("nurture and admonition" in the KJV), as they work under the authority of their husbands. This responsibility is invoked in Paul's description of a godly widow, for she was to have "brought up children" herself (1 Timothy 5:10). In this way, a godly mother is a delegate of her husband in the matter of teaching their children, and they together must share the task of educating their children in their home.

As you now prepare to teach your children at home, take on this motherly work by employing both discipline and instruction. To exercise discipline, you must apply physical direction and correction as a part of your children's education. For your homeschool to succeed, you will have to establish your authority as a parent and remind your children of it when needed. It is your children's obligation to obey you, as the Scripture says, "Children, obey your par-

---

[124] See Chapter 20, "Letter to Fathers."

ents in the Lord, for this is right" (Ephesians 6:1; also Colossians 3:20). This God-given maternal authority is exemplified in the Law of Moses, which said, "If any man has a stubborn and rebellious son who will not obey his father or his mother, and when they chastise him, he will not even listen to them, then his father and mother shall seize him, and bring him out to the elders of his city at the gateway of his hometown" (Deuteronomy 21:18-19). This authority is also evident in Proverbs 29:15, which says, "The rod and reproof give wisdom, but a child who gets his own way brings shame to his mother." Even the Lord Himself was in subjection to His own mother as she had authority over the child Jesus (Luke 2:51).

Of course, the majority of the education that you give to your children will come in the form of instruction. Verbal instruction will likely be the main mode of your homeschool, whether it comes from you or your husband. The Scriptures equally extol the instructions of both a father and a mother. To this point, consider a few verses from the Proverbs:

> Hear, my son, your father's instruction, and do not forsake your mother's teaching; indeed, they are a graceful wreath to your head and ornaments about your neck. (Proverbs 1:8-9).

> My son, observe the commandment of your father, and do not forsake the teaching of your mother; bind them continually on your heart; tie them around your neck. (Proverbs 6:20-21).

> The words of King Lemuel, the oracle which his mother taught him: What, O my son? And what, O son of my womb? And what, O son of my vows? (Proverbs 31:1-2)

This last passage from Proverbs 31 is especially interesting because we learn that an inspired mother provided the description of an excellent wife given in verses 10-31. Among the esteemed qualities of an excellent wife that were taught to King Lemuel by his mother is that which is taught in verse 26, "She opens her mouth in wisdom, and the teaching of kindness is on her tongue." When you speak to your children in wise and kind instruction, you will fulfill God's intent for you as an excellent wife and mother, just as King Lemuel's mother did when she taught him.

A mother's teachings can be so effective that even when a father fails to nurture his child in the discipline and instruction of the Lord, a mother's lessons can make up for that failure. Timothy is an example of one who was well taught because of his faithful mother (and grandmother). Timothy was the son of a believing Jewish mother and an unbelieving Greek father (Acts 16:1). He became a believer in Christ and a faithful evangelist largely because of the faithful, Scriptural teachings of his mother and grandmother from his childhood. Notice Paul's words to Timothy about the faithful women of his life:

> For I am mindful of **the sincere faith within you, which first dwelt in your grandmother Lois and your mother Eunice**, and I am sure that it is in you as well. (2 Timothy 1:5)

> You, however, continue in the things you have learned and become convinced of, **knowing from whom you have learned them, and that from childhood you have known the sacred writings** which are able to give you the wisdom that leads to salvation through faith which is in Christ Jesus. (2 Timothy 3:14-15)

From Timothy's earliest days, his mother and grandmother had faithfully instructed him in "the sacred writings," namely, the Scripture which "is inspired by God and profitable for teaching, for reproof, for correction, for training in righteousness; so that the man of God may be adequate, equipped for every good work" (2 Timothy 3:16-17). Just as Lois and Eunice educated Timothy in God's word, so also many other godly mothers have taught their sons and daughters God's word, and some did so even without the help of their children's fathers.

I said before that many women have been convinced that the home is too small of a place for them, but actually the world is too small to satisfy the aspirations of a godly woman whose ambition for herself and her family is heaven. For such a woman, no amount of worldly success or money could be enough to compensate her without the satisfaction of seeing her children walk with the Lord. Likewise, no amount of worldly acclaim could be enough to replace the praise of her family, for "her children rise up and bless her; her husband also, and he praises her, saying: 'Many daughters have done nobly, but you excel them all'" (Proverbs 31:28-29). Most of all, nothing in this world can replace the reward of her God who will bless her eternally for faithfully embracing the work He gave to her. Indeed, the world cannot offer a woman the blessings of a godly home.

Dear mothers, I hope that these words from the Scriptures have reinforced your decision to homeschool and encouraged you to proceed without hesitation. There is no doubt that you will be blessed for every effort you make to educate your children in a way to cultivate faithfulness to God within them. By selecting this course, you are embracing the wisdom of God concerning women and motherhood and shunning the foolish ways of the world. Your children, your home, and you will be better because of your faithful service. May God bless you chosen ladies and your children (2 John 1).

Regards in the Lord,
Stacey

22

A Letter for Your Children

Dear Christian Parents and your Children,

Let me begin by speaking to you parents and saying that I don't really expect for your children to read this letter themselves. However, I want to address most of my comments to your children because homeschooling is all about them. Therefore, I ask you fathers and mothers to read this letter aloud to your children or else explain it to them in your own terms that are appropriate for their ages. Through this letter and the Scriptures, I hope to help your children understand why their education and upbringing will be different from that of many others. I also want them to understand their part in your family's homeschool.

Now I want to speak directly to the children and young people who are to be educated by their own parents at home. To them I ask this question: Do you know that you are God's gift to your parents? The Bible says so in Psalm 127:3 – "Behold, children are a gift of the LORD, the fruit of the womb is a reward." How does that make you feel about yourself? If you are not humble in heart, then you might become proud and arrogant about being God's gift. You might think that your parents owe it to you to give you anything you want and to treat you like a king or queen. However, if you are humble and godly in spirit, then you will realize that as a gift to your parents you have a responsibility to them. God intended for you to be a blessing to your parents, so you must try to live up to God's intentions.

Because you are a gift to your parents, you should make it your goal to bring joy to your father and mother. After all, no gift should ever bring grief to its owners, but instead it should make them happy. Notice what the Bible says about your parents' happiness in Proverbs 23:24-25:

> The father of the righteous will greatly rejoice,
> And he who sires a wise son will be glad in him.
> Let your father and your mother be glad,
> And let her rejoice who gave birth to you.

This passage of Scripture shows that you will bring joy to your parents by becoming righteous and wise. As a father myself, I know this is true because of my own experience with my children. I pray that every Christian father and mother will have such happiness and be able to say, "I have no greater joy than this, to hear of my children walking in the truth" (3 John 4). Of course, I know that you want to bring the greatest joy to your parents, and thankfully God has given you this ability as their precious gift.

When you try to bring joy to your parents, wonderful things will happen for you. Not only will your father and mother be made happy, but God also will be pleased with you. The Bible says, "Children, be obedient to your parents in all things, for this is well-pleasing to the Lord" (Colossians 3:20). When you obey your parents, you are fulfilling God's will for you as children, and this will lead to many blessings for you. Notice the promise given to you in Ephesians 6:1-3 – "Children, obey your parents in the Lord, for this is right. Honor your father and mother (which is the first commandment with a promise), so that it may be well with you, and that you may live long on the earth." When you honor God by honoring your parents, God gives you His promise that it will "be well with you." In this way, you not only make your parents happy, but you also make yourself happy.

What does all of this have to do with homeschooling? The answer is everything. Homeschooling is the best method of education for you to achieve your joy, your parents' joy, and most importantly the joy of God. When your parents educate you at home, they are following God's plan for bringing you up in the "discipline and instruction of the Lord" (Ephesians 6:4). They are following the Bible's pattern for teaching you God's word "when you sit in your house and when you walk by the way and when you lie down and when you rise up" (Deuteronomy 6:7; 11:19). They are training you up in the way you should go so that when you are old you will not depart from it (Proverbs 22:6). They are doing their very best to instruct you in righteousness, wisdom, and truth so that all of you may share the joy of the Lord.

Not only are your parents teaching you these good things through homeschooling, but also they are saving you from many evil things. They are keeping you from the counsel of the wicked, the path of sinners, and the seats of scoffers (Psalm 1:1). They are sparing you from the harm that comes from foolish companions (Proverbs 13:20). They are protecting you from blind teachers who are not even allowed to speak of God or teach from the Bible in public schools (Luke 6:39-40). If your parents did not choose to educate you at home, then all of these things would be working against you.

Your parents have chosen to homeschool you because they "want you to be wise in what is good and innocent in what is evil" (Romans 16:19). Because your father and mother want to be certain that you learn all that is good, right, and true, they have taken on the job of teaching you themselves. Their goal for your education is not just for you to learn math, science, English, and other subjects, but rather it is for you to become faithful to God throughout your life. They know that you are a precious gift from God, so they are treating you like a treasure inherited from the Lord. Just as you would keep a valuable treasure in a safe place where it would not be stolen or damaged, so also your parents are keeping you in the safety of your home and family so that your heart will not be stolen or damaged. How blessed you are to have such loving, godly parents!

Now that you understand what your parents want to accomplish through homeschool, let's focus on what you must do. As we saw before in Ephesians 6:1-3 and Colossians 3:20, your responsibility toward your parents begins with honor and obedience. To honor your father and mother, you must have great respect for them and consider them to be very important. God has made them to be your parents, so your honor for them is also honor for God. When you have a proper sense of honor for both your parents and God, obedience to your parents will not be difficult for you. You will naturally do as they tell you to do. It is only when your sense of honor begins to fail that you will disobey your parents. Be warned that God counts disobedience to parents as one of the worst offenses a person can commit (Deuteronomy 21:18-21; Romans 1:28-

32; 2 Timothy 3:1-5). Guard yourself against this, and you will do well.

In every part of your life, it is very important that you always listen carefully to your parents. This is especially true in your family's homeschool because your parents will be giving constant instructions, lessons, and teachings. The Bible is filled with messages for you about the importance of listening to your father and your mother. Let's read a few of those messages from the Proverbs and think about how they apply to your responsibility in your family's homeschool.

> The fear of the LORD is the beginning of knowledge; fools despise wisdom and instruction. Hear, my son, your father's instruction and do not forsake your mother's teaching; indeed, they are a graceful wreath to your head and ornaments about your neck. (Proverbs 1:7-9)

> My son, do not forget my teaching, but let your heart keep my commandments; for length of days and years of life and peace they will add to you. (Proverbs 3:1-2)

> Hear, O sons, the instruction of a father, and give attention that you may gain understanding, for I give you sound teaching; do not abandon my instruction. When I was a son to my father, tender and the only son in the sight of my mother, then he taught me and said to me, "Let your heart hold fast my words; keep my commandments and live..." (Proverbs 4:1-4)

> Hear, my son, and accept my sayings and the years of your life will be many. I have directed you in the way of wisdom; I have led you in upright paths. When you walk, your steps will not be impeded; and if you run, you will not stumble. Take hold of instruction; do not let go. Guard her, for she is your life. (Proverbs 4:10-13)

> My son, observe the commandment of your father and do not forsake the teaching of your mother; bind them continually on your heart; tie them around your neck. When you walk about, they will guide you; when you sleep, they will watch over you; and when you awake, they will talk to you. (Proverbs 6:20-22)

Listen to your father who begot you, and do not despise your mother when she is old. (Proverbs 23:22)

Did you notice how many blessings are promised in these Scripture passages? If you listen to your father and mother, then your life will be better in every way. How blessed you are because you are homeschooled and get to listen to your parents all the time! Another responsibility you have in your family life and home-school is to accept your parents' discipline. Discipline is an unpleasant but necessary part of life for children whose parents love them. The Bible says, "He who withholds his rod hates his son, but he who loves him disciplines him diligently" (Proverbs 13:24). When you receive discipline from your parents, try to understand that they are loving you. Also, try to keep in mind the purpose of discipline, which is explained in Hebrews 12:11 – "All discipline for the moment seems not to be joyful, but sorrowful; yet to those who have been trained by it, afterwards it yields the peaceful fruit of righteousness." You must believe that your parents discipline you because they love you, they know it is good for you, and they know it trains you in righteousness.

Therefore, you must obediently accept discipline without resisting. I know this is not easy, but when you know that it is right and for your own good, you will humble yourself and submit to your parents. The Bible has much to say about those who accept discipline and those who reject it. Let's read a few of these Bible passages, and then you can decide for yourself whether you should accept or resist discipline.

My son, do not reject the discipline of the LORD or loathe His reproof, for whom the LORD loves He reproves, even as a father corrects the son in whom he delights. (Proverbs 3:11-12)

A wise son accepts his father's discipline, but a scoffer does not listen to rebuke. (Proverbs 13:1)

A fool rejects his father's discipline, but he who regards reproof is sensible. (Proverbs 15:5)

Cease listening, my son, to discipline, and you will stray from the words of knowledge. (Proverbs 19:27)

> Foolishness is bound up in the heart of a child; the rod of discipline will remove it far from him. (Proverbs 22:15)

The choice for you is simple. You may accept discipline from your parents and be made wise, or you may reject discipline and be foolish. No one wants to be a fool, so accept discipline and be wise.

By honoring your parents, obeying them, listening carefully to their instruction, and accepting their discipline, you can realize your true potential through homeschooling. Do you know what your potential is? The word "potential" means the possibility of achieving something. What achievements can your parents help you reach by teaching you at home? Let's list a few of the most important goals.

- You can "remember...your Creator in the days of your youth..." (Ecclesiastes 12:1). The godly education your parents give you will always keep you in mind of God.
- You can learn the Bible early in your life just as Timothy did. The apostle Paul said to him, "...from childhood you have known the sacred writings which are able to give you the wisdom that leads to salvation through faith which is in Christ Jesus" (2 Timothy 3:15). Timothy learned the Bible from his mother and grandmother (2 Timothy 1:5), and your parents will teach you just as well.
- You can learn to serve God from a very young age. Even small children can bring glory to God, for the children shouted to Jesus in the temple, "Hosanna to the Son of David!" (Matthew 21:15-16). Likewise, when Samuel was very young, his mother took him to the house of the Lord where he worshipped God (1 Samuel 1:25-28). Your parents will also teach you how to serve the Lord from your youth, and that good training will last throughout your life.

These goals are good and honorable in the sight of God. All of these are within your potential, and your parents have chosen homeschooling as the best way to educate you for reaching that potential. How blessed you are for having parents that care so much for you!

Maybe you are wondering about math, science, English, history, and all of those other subjects. How do they fit into your family's homeschool? You will learn all of those subjects and more in the very best way possible because your parents will teach you according to God's word. You will be blessed to learn all things with the fear of God, for "the fear of the LORD is the beginning of wisdom, and the knowledge of the Holy One is understanding" (Proverbs 9:10). Your understanding of all things will be much better than it would be if you were taught in an ordinary public school because you will know God's truth about all subjects. How truly blessed you are!

Now you know all about your parents' reasons for home-schooling you, and you understand your responsibilities. You know the blessings that are in store for you because your parents love both you and God enough to educate you at home. You are also beginning to know the joy of having godly parents as they also experience the joy of having godly children. I hope that you will always remember these things, and I pray that you and your family will have the greatest success in homeschooling. May God bless you and your family.

Regards in the Lord,
Stacey

23

A Letter to Prospective Parents

Dear "Prospective" Christian Parents,

I realize that there may be some of you reading these letters who do not yet have children. If that is the case for you, then you are reading because you are concerned for "the generation to come" and "the children yet to be born" (Psalms 78:6; 102:18). I commend you for your forethought regarding your future family, for it reveals the godly values treasured within your heart. Because children and family are important to you, it is not too early for you to start thinking about your children and planning to raise them up for the Lord. Getting a head start on your family plans is a great advantage for you, so I offer this letter to help you become the best prepared parents you can be.

If you are not yet married, then you are already far ahead of the curve regarding homeschooling. Most unmarried people have given little or no serious thought to children at all, and they almost certainly have not studied up on homeschooling. You, however, are showing uncommon wisdom, and I expect that you will do the same in selecting a spouse.

Of course, your choice of spouse will be critical to the success of homeschooling in your family. If you choose a spouse who doesn't share your Christian values and views of children's education, then you will have trouble not only in homeschool but also in marriage in general. I cannot emphasize enough the importance of marrying a Christian. The Bible is filled with examples and warnings concerning unbelieving and ungodly spouses (see 1 Samuel 25; 1 Kings 11:1-3; 16:31; 21:25; Proverbs 21:9, 19; 25:24; 27:15-16). Consider Samson, who wanted a Philistine woman for his bride.

When his parents asked, "Is there no woman among the daughters of your relatives, or among all our people, that you go to take a wife from the uncircumcised Philistines?" he replied, "Get her for me, for she looks good to me" (Judges 14:3). In the likeness of Samson, too many Christians choose spouses based on appearances or other temporal qualities, and they suffer for their foolish choices just as Samson did. Moreover, the children born into such marriages suffer because of the spiritual division of their parents. You can avoid this trouble by selecting a spouse who shares your faith in Christ. Try to view your potential spouse as God would, "for God sees not as man sees, for man looks at the outward appearance, but the LORD looks at the heart" (1 Samuel 16:7).

I expect that most of you who are reading this letter are already married, so I will address the remainder of my comments primarily to the married. My advice regarding homeschooling for all prospective parents in Christ can be summarized in this instruction: Don't put yourself in a position now that will prevent you from homeschooling your children later. There are many snares that can trap you into such a position, so it is best to be aware of them and to avoid them before you get caught. This is easier said than done, but if you heed the teachings of God's word, then you will avoid the pitfalls while preparing yourselves for God's blessings.

The best way to prepare for children and homeschooling is to perfect your marriage. I don't mean that your marriage has to be perfect in the sense of being flawless, but rather I mean that it should be complete, whole, and mature. Once you are married, you need to quickly master the roles of husband and wife. Hopefully, even before you were married, you studied God's design for marriage in the Biblical model and now have a full understanding of what your respective roles as husbands and wives should be. Go back and read passages of Scripture such as these: Genesis 1:26-28; 2:18-25; 3:16-19; 9:1; Proverbs 5:15-23; 31:1-31; Matthew 19:4-6; Ephesians 5:22-33; Colossians 3:18-19; Titus 2:4-5; Hebrews 13:4; 1 Peter 3:1-7. Every husband must apply these passages by exercising leadership and authority over his wife with a Christ-like love and gentleness. Every wife must apply them by submitting to her husband in love as a divinely appointed helper. If you both will let the word of God completely govern your marriage, then you will do well.

When you have a godly marriage, you will be well prepared to welcome children into your home and raise them up in the Lord. Hopefully for you, God will open the womb quickly and bless you with His precious gift (Psalm 127:3). For this reason, you should waste no time in perfecting your marriage, for it will be the bedrock institution of your family and your children. An older friend of mine once told me, "When you get married, it's a drop in the bucket. When you have children, it's the rest of the bucket." By this, he meant that if you struggle with marriage, then you will be absolutely overwhelmed with children. Therefore, get your marriage relationships right immediately so that you will be ready for children, and pray that God will give you children soon.

Part of having a godly marriage is managing your household well, and this is where many of the obstacles to homeschooling can be avoided. Making wise, godly choices for your marriage and home will prepare you for the arrival of children and put you in a position to homeschool them. On the other hand, making foolish choices can trap you in a situation that may snowball out of control. The Bible says, "He who troubles his own house will inherit wind, and the foolish will be servant to the wisehearted" (Proverbs 11:29). How can we expect God to bless us with the precious inheritance of children if we bring trouble to our own households by mismanagement and ungodly choices?

Let me share a personal example with you. When I worked as an engineer, some of my coworkers would say to me, "You are so lucky that your wife can stay at home." They envied the fact that my wife stayed at home with our children while their wives worked outside of the home. They would talk about how they wished they could afford for their wives to stay at home. They would say, "My wife has to work," as if my wife and I were independently wealthy and she was a woman of leisure (ha!). It seemed to them to be pure luck for me that we worked at the same place and earned similar salaries, but somehow my wife could afford to stay at home while theirs could not. Was it luck?

It wasn't luck, but rather it was choice. My wife and I had chosen to use God's word to guide our decisions about our marriage, our family, and our home. As a result, we had discovered that "godliness is profitable for all things" (1 Timothy 4:7-8). That didn't mean that God miraculously sent more money to us because my wife stayed at home. In fact, our family had less money, a smaller house, cheaper cars, less fashionable clothes, etc. than many of my coworkers' families, but we always had everything we needed. We had learned that "godliness actually is a means of great gain when accompanied by contentment" (1 Timothy 6:6; see also Philippians 4:11). This was no credit to me or my wife, but rather it was the providence of God and the wisdom of His word.

For this reason and many others in my experience, I can personally testify of God's kind blessings that come providentially through obedience to His word. This is why I encourage you also to follow His wisdom in this season of your lives so that you will be ready for the next season when children hopefully come. Don't count on "luck" to make things happen, but trust in God by proactively choosing to follow His word.

Specifically, I urge you not to become accustomed to an extravagant lifestyle that requires two incomes to sustain it. It is too easy to become slaves of an expensive way of life and unable to adjust when needed. For example, if you buy a large, expensive house that requires both of you to work to pay for it, then what will you do when children come? You could sell the house and downsize, but that will be difficult when you are expanding your family and need the extra space more than ever. You will likely find yourselves trapped in the same predicament as my old coworkers with you husbands saying, "My wife has to work to pay the bills." This will make it very difficult to homeschool in the future, and, worse still, it may even hinder your ability to follow Christ (Luke 18:18-27). For this reason, I encourage all couples with or without children to live on the husband's income only and find a way to make it work.

If you don't follow the wisdom of God's word in managing your household with restraint and moderation, then you will likely fall into one of the deepest pits of all, which is debt. Debt is probably the most common factor that prevents Christian mothers who want to stay at home with their children from doing so. It breaks my heart to see so many young Christian couples begin their marriages with a deluge of debt in the form of student loans, home mortgages, loans for new cars, and credit cards. They plunge into this debt without realizing that they are basically selling their unborn children's futures for their own present gratification. They remind me of the post-exilic Jews, who said, "We are forcing our sons and our daughters to be slaves, and some of our daughters are forced into bondage already, and we are helpless because our fields and vineyards belong to others" (Nehemiah 5:5). In the case of these young Christian couples, their children will likely become slaves of the public school system because of their debt.

You don't have to follow this sad trend of becoming enslaved to debt, for the Bible gives you ample warning against it. The Scripture says, "The rich rules over the poor, and the borrower becomes the lender's slave" (Proverbs 22:7; see Leviticus 25:39, 47). For this reason, Christians are commanded, "Owe nothing to anyone except to love one another..." (Romans 13:8). The Lord Jesus used the example of two debtors to teach a lesson on forgiveness in Matthew 18:23-35, but His lesson also reveals the terrible price of debt as wives and children are sold into bondage because of it. While debt may be a way of life here in our nation, it has never garnered the favor and blessings of God.

If you are already in debt, then make every effort to get out of it. In Proverbs 6:1-5, a man caught in debt is advised to do everything he can to make himself free. He is to humbly beg to be released from his debt and to work sleeplessly until he obtains his liberty (see also vv. 6-11 that follow). You likewise would be wise to do whatever you can lawfully, ethically, and morally to pay off your debts and be free as soon as you can. "Deliver yourself like a gazelle from the hunter's hand and like a bird from the hand of the fowler" (v. 5). Otherwise, you are putting yourself at a terrible disadvantage for raising children and having any hopes of homeschooling them.

Regarding all money issues and debt, the best advice I can give you is simply to commend the following passage of Scripture to you. I mentioned part of it before, but here is the whole message of 1 Timothy 6:6-10:

> But godliness actually is a means of great gain when accompanied by contentment. For we have brought nothing into the world, so we cannot take anything out of it either. If we have food and covering, with these we shall be content. But those who want to get rich fall into temptation and a snare and many foolish and harmful desires which plunge men into ruin and destruction. For the love of money is a root of all sorts of evil, and some by longing for it have wandered away from the faith and pierced themselves with many griefs.

Notice the terms "snare," "foolish and harmful desires," "ruin and destruction," "all sorts of evil," and "many griefs." These are indicative of the trouble that comes to your household when you make unwise decisions about money, and how much greater is that trouble when it affects children. It is far better to avoid these troubles altogether beforehand rather than having to struggle to escape them later.

Otherwise, my advice to you prospective Christian parents is the same as that which I have given to parents in the other letters I have written. Read all of these letters, and use the time you now have as an advantage to get fully prepared for children and homeschooling. Go ahead and apply the first two steps of "A Plan for Homeschooling"[125] by loving God with all your heart, with all your soul, and with all your might and stamping God's word onto your heart. I know that God will bless you for your efforts. Indeed, may He bless you to "be fruitful and multiply" (Genesis 1:28; 9:7), and may your quiver be full of arrows (Psalm 127:4-5).

Regards in the Lord,
Stacey

---

[125] See Chapter 17.

24

Don't Grow Weary

Dear Christian Parents,

We have come a long way and addressed many issues in these letters, but now I want to consider one more category of topics that is essential to the success of your homeschool. I am speaking of patience, endurance, steadfastness, perseverance, persistence, constancy, forbearance, longsuffering...you get the idea. Homeschooling is a long road to travel, so both you and your children will need these traits to make it to the end. Don't get me wrong – the journey of homeschooling children is a joy, but you will encounter bumps in the road along the way. I want to help you get through those rough spots without ever giving up.

For Christian parents, the best role model of parenting is always found in our heavenly Parent, God the Father. Consider how amazingly patient the Father is with us, His children. He is "compassionate and gracious, slow to anger, and abounding in lovingkindness" (Exodus 34:6) even when we have been stubborn, rebellious, sinful, and deserving of His wrath and punishment. His kindness, forbearance, and patience are immeasurably rich blessings that lead us to repentance (Romans 2:4). His patience toward us is the opportunity for salvation that would otherwise be impossible (2 Peter 3:9, 15). Let us praise and thank our Father in heaven for suffering so long with us.

With the example of your heavenly Father before you, apply your experience with Him to your relationship with your own children. Now you are the parent who must lovingly and patiently suffer the youthful shortcomings of your children, such as instances of stubbornness, rebellion, disobedience, ignorance, disrespect, and insolence. In these situations, your patience toward your children should mirror the patience of your heavenly Father toward you. He has never run out of patience with you, and neither should you be short on patience with your children.

There will certainly be times when your children will provoke your anger, but your love for them must rule those moments just as God's love has governed His dealings with you. Rather than reacting to youthful indiscretions with wrath, love will lead you to discipline and train your children with an even hand (Proverbs 3:12; 13:24; 19:18; 22:6, 15; 23:13-14; 29:15, 17; Ephesians 6:4). Likewise, rather than using hurtful words and a raised voice, love will constrain you to speak to your children in gentle firmness and conviction. Remember, "Everyone must be quick to hear, slow to speak and slow to anger; for the anger of man does not achieve the righteousness of God" (James 1:19-20).

Consider carefully the words and tones you use with your children in those moments of anger. There is an old song that says, "You always hurt the one you love," and in many families this is true. I have heard parents say things to their own children that they would never say to anyone else. These parents would not allow others to speak to their children in such hateful ways, so why would they do it? There should be no place for cruel words or screaming in parents' communication with their children. Fathers especially need to remember the charge given to them in the first part of Ephesians 6:4 – "Do not provoke your children to anger..." You cannot keep this charge when railing against your children, for "a gentle answer turns away wrath, but a harsh word stirs up anger" (Proverbs 15:1). Your little children may throw tantrums at some point, but don't teach them how to do so by your own undisciplined manner.

There is a passage of Scripture that can be very helpful for homeschool parents and teachers, although the primary purpose is not about parenting. This passage is 2 Timothy 2:24-26:

> The Lord's bond-servant must not be quarrelsome, but be kind to all, able to teach, patient when wronged, with gentleness correcting those who are in opposition, if perhaps God may grant them repentance leading to the knowledge of the truth, and they may come to their senses and escape from the snare of the devil, having been held captive by him to do his will.

Notice a few of the characteristics from this passage that you need to have as a godly teacher of your children. You shouldn't be quarrelsome by arguing with your children. Remember that as the authority over your children, you do not have to explain everything you do, so don't be drawn into pointless debates with them. Also, be patient when your children offend you. Understand that these things happen with children, and then deal with them appropriately in forbearance. Furthermore, correct your children with gentleness when they are in opposition to you or to God. Your response to such situations must be unequivocal correction, but deliver that correction with as much gentleness as the situation allows. The result will be godly sorrow on the part of your children that leads them to amend their behavior.

Most of what I have said about patience so far pertains to day-to-day situations that will arise in your home, but let's also consider the endurance that you need for the long term. Homeschooling is an endurance race of family education, and it will require real fortitude to cross the finish line. You will likely be tried by doubt from within, ridicule from without, weariness, frustration, failure, and other obstacles along the way, but all the trouble will be worth the effort when you realize your greatest joy of seeing your children walk in truth (3 John 4).

Therefore, I urge you not to wear yourself out in the pursuit of education. Some homeschool families have suffered burnout, which is fatigue, frustration, or apathy that results from overwork. This can happen when parents and children are so eager to succeed that they become overzealous and too intense. Their initial burst of energy and enthusiasm soon gives way to dread and lethargy. Guard yourself against this, for it will derail you from your goal and tempt you to give up.

To avoid burnout, approach your homeschool with sensible moderation. Academically, don't take on too much. There is a tendency among some homeschoolers to push their children to the extreme limits of their abilities. There is nothing wrong with wanting your children to reach the fullness of their capabilities, but that can be accomplished without breaking their spirits. Be reasonable in your expectations of them. They don't have to win the national spelling bee, become fluent in Latin, or have proficiency in integral calculus by age twelve. Be mindful of the admonition of Solomon, who wrote, "But beyond this, my son, be warned: the writing of many books is endless, and excessive devotion to books is wearying to the body" (Ecclesiastes 12:12).

Likewise, don't spend too much time chasing your children's education in your car. Some homeschool parents spend so much time going from place to place with their children that they are rarely at home. Every day they are going to study at the library, see a play at the theater, hear a concert at the music hall, play soccer at the park, take a piano lesson at the music teacher's house, learn to swim at the civic center, or participate in some other worthy activity. At some point, constantly going here and there becomes exhausting and counterproductive. Too much time on the road can be stifling for children, and too many irons in the fire can become unmanageable for you. Scale back these activities, and you will reduce the stress on your whole family without compromising your children's education. Be assured that there will be plenty of time for your children to learn and experience everything they need to know for life and godliness (2 Peter 1:3).

When frustration arises in your homeschool, you need to take time to address it. Frustrated children tend to shut down mentally and become incapable of learning. If you and your children become frustrated, then you will accomplish very little. Take a break and figure out what is wrong. Frustration is a symptom of some underlying problem, so determine the cause of the frustration, and do what is necessary to resolve it. Ask yourself some questions: Is the lesson too hard for the child? Are you trying to do too much? Is something wrong with the child or with you (lack of rest, distractions, unrelated problems)? Is the problem in your child's attitude so that you need to set aside the academic lesson and teach a character lesson? Is the problem in your attitude? When you find the cause of the problem, get it solved and move on. Usually, a healthy dose of the fruit of the spirit (love, joy, peace, patience, kindness, goodness, faithfulness, gentleness, and self-control — Galatians 5:22-23) will do the trick.

To further combat burnout, try some variety in your homeschool. Mix it up. Don't follow the same routine every day. Give your children plenty of breaks from their studies, and send them outside often. Boys especially are not wired for sitting at a desk for hours at a time. Try changing your schedule to have school four days each week instead of five days by shortening your summer break. Have special studies that last for only one or two weeks.

Use different methods to teach different subjects. For example, don't use fill-in-the-blank workbooks for every subject, but instead provide some variety for your children. Take advantage of the many different ways of presenting information to them — books, videos, audio CDs, hands-on experiments, computer software, creative projects, etc. All of these assorted approaches will help prevent burnout, frustration, and weariness in your homeschool. Be creative, and keep things lively and interesting.

Finally, find what works for your family and do it. One of the great benefits of homeschooling is that you can customize your children's education to suit them. Rather than the Horace Mann style of one-size-fits-all education that dominates the public school, your homeschool can vary even from child to child. In fact, your homeschool may be completely different from some other family's homeschool, yet both can be equally effective for the respective families. This freedom to customize your approach will help to maintain your energy and enthusiasm while preventing burnout and fatigue.

The best advice I can give you regarding endurance for your homeschool is simply a few words of encouragement from the Bible. Here are a few verses of Scripture to help edify you for persevering in the endurance race you have chosen to run.

Trust in the LORD with all your heart and do not lean on your own understanding. In all your ways acknowledge Him, and He will make your paths straight. (Proverbs 3:5-6)

Let us not lose heart in doing good, for in due time we will reap if we do not grow weary. (Galatians 6:9)

But as for you, brethren, do not grow weary of doing good. (2 Thessalonians 3:13)

Do you not know that those who run in a race all run, but only one receives the prize? Run in such a way that you may win. (1 Corinthians 9:24)

For you have need of endurance, so that when you have done the will of God, you may receive what was promised. (Hebrews 10:36)

For consider Him who has endured such hostility by sinners against Himself, so that you will not grow weary and lose heart. (Hebrews 12:3)

Therefore humble yourselves under the mighty hand of God, that He may exalt you at the proper time, casting all your anxiety on Him, because He cares for you. (1 Peter 5:6-7)

Truly, if you trust in God, stay the course, and finish the race, then the reward for you and your children will be great. I pray that your resolve and faith will be strong so that you may realize your goals and rewards in full. May God bless you and your family.

Regards in the Lord,
Stacey

25

I Commend You to God and His Word

Dear Christian Parents,

"And now I commend you to God and to the word of His grace, which is able to build you up and to give you the inheritance among all those who are sanctified" (Acts 20:32). These are the words of the apostle Paul spoken to the elders of the church of Ephesus as they had a final, tearful goodbye. What better way to part than to commend the brethren to God and His word?

Now as I write a final letter to you, I leave you with this same godly commendation. My ambition throughout these letters has been to "commend you to God and to the word of His grace" in the matter of your children's education. Although there are many ostensible experts on children and many theories about education, only God and His word are truly commendable guides for Christian families to follow. Our Creator knows what is best for His children, and He has communicated His will for their education through the Bible. This is what I have commended to you.

In my parting words to you, I want to "stir you up by way of reminder" of the truth I have presented to you so that "you will be able to call these things to mind" (2 Peter 1:13, 15). I hope that you will remember all that I have had to say, but here again I give you what I consider to be some of the most significant and convincing points from my previous letters:

- The most important purpose for the education of children is to cultivate faithfulness to God within them. If education fails to do this, then it is worthless, for it fails to prepare them for the very purpose of life (Ecclesiastes 12:13; Hebrews 11:6).

- In education as in all things, when you seek first the kingdom of God and His righteousness, God will provide all that you need (Matt 6:32-33; 7:7-11). Therefore, pursue the good and right way for your children's education, and be assured of your success.

- Your children are a gift, a heritage, and an inheritance from God to you (Psalm 127:3-5). They are a treasure and stewardship entrusted to your care, and it is your responsibility to aim them at godly targets and give them godly goals. Without a doubt, education is a large part of that responsibility.

- The Bible reveals a pattern for educating children (Deuteronomy 6:4-9), and God-centered homeschooling fits that pattern better than any other model for teaching children. If you intend to follow the Biblical pattern for educating your children, then homeschooling is the right choice for you.

- There is no better place than a God-centered home for imparting wisdom, understanding, and knowledge to children (Proverbs 24:3-4). Your children need to be at home with you, and you need to be with them.

- There is no greater joy for Christian parents than to see their children walking in truth (3 John 4). No other achievement will make you as happy as your children's spiritual success. Therefore, do all you can to realize your greatest joy.

- Studies show that you have a 94 percent chance of passing your faith in Christ on to your children when you educate them at home. On the other hand, you have about an 85 percent chance of failure when you send your children to public school. If your goal is to cultivate faithfulness to God in your children, then the decision to homeschool should be settled by these odds of success.

- The original intent of education in America was to promote religion, morality, and knowledge, but now public schools are legally barred from providing anything other than a secular humanist education for children. These schools will not only fail to cultivate faith in your children, but they will also likely hinder your children from having faith in God.

- Homeschooling is a legal alternative to compulsory schools throughout America. Laws governing homeschooling vary from state to state, but the U.S. Supreme Court has repeatedly upheld and defended parents' fundamental rights to educate their children.

- Compulsory government schools are consumed with corrupt philosophies and are getting worse. Christians can act discreetly, wisely, shrewdly, and innocently to comply with compulsory school laws by avoiding the public schools altogether and educating their own children at home.

- God's first provision for the socialization of man was marriage and the family (Genesis 1:27-28; 2:18-24), and this is still the best design. Daily interaction with parents, siblings, and extended family members will be more than enough to give your children the social skills that God intended. Of course, you may provide as much socialization for your children outside the family as you see fit.

- You will bless your children if you keep them from the ungodly socialization found in the public schools (Psalm 1:1; Proverbs 13:20; 18:24; 1 Corinthians 15:33). Protect your children from the influence of bad company, and don't worry about sheltering them too much.

- If you follow God's plan from the Scriptures for educating your children from birth to adulthood (Deuteronomy 6:4-9), then the well-being of your children will be great (Isaiah 54:13). Start early, stick to the plan, and finish strong.

- The word of God must be the basis from which all education flows, for "the fear of the LORD is the beginning of wisdom, and the knowledge of the Holy One is understanding" (Proverbs 9:10). Teach all subjects in your homeschool with a Biblical worldview, and your children will have a truly good education.

- Fathers, mothers, and children all need to understand their roles in the home and in homeschool. The better these roles are understood and followed, the greater the success of your homeschool will be.

- Don't grow weary or lose heart in your homeschool, but learn patience and have endurance for the sake of your children (Galatians 6:9; Hebrews 10:36; 12:3). Be like your heavenly Father, who never grows weary or impatient of you.

These points form the foundation of my Biblical appeal to you for homeschooling. At length, I have expounded on these matters in my letters to you, and now once more I ask you to take on the vital task of educating your own children for yourself. With fervent prayer and careful study, commit yourself to this worthy endeavor for your children, and you will never regret it. "Commit your works to the LORD and your plans will be established" (Proverbs 16:3).

While I remind you of these points, I also want to emphasize the final outcome. Education is a means to an end, but what will that end be for your children? For you Christian parents, the goal of educating your children should not be temporal in nature. Your primary motivation shouldn't be to see your children graduate summa cum laude, embark on a prestigious career, and make lots of money, although these accomplishments may result as distant, secondary achievements. Instead, your goal should be to spiritually prepare your children to emerge from this world with their souls preserved for eternity by the grace of God through faith in Christ Jesus. This is why I have said time and time again that my goal is to convince you to educate your children in the best way to cultivate faithfulness to God within them.

Therefore, it is appropriate to end these letters by commending you again to "God and the word of His grace," for only they can "give you the inheritance among all those who are sanctified." Concerning this inheritance, consider the words of Scripture from 1 Peter 1:3-5 (emphasis added):

Blessed be the God and Father of our Lord Jesus Christ, who according to His great mercy has caused us to be born again to a living hope through the resurrection of Jesus Christ from the dead, to obtain **an inheritance which is imperishable and undefiled and will not fade away, reserved in heaven for you,** who are protected by the power of God through faith for a salvation ready to be revealed in the last time.

What will be the inheritance of your children? Will they grow up to be "born again not of seed which is perishable but imperishable, that is, through the living and enduring word of God" (1 Peter

1:23)? Will they "obtain an inheritance which is imperishable and undefiled and will not fade away, reserved in heaven"? Will they be "of those who have faith to the preserving of the soul" (Hebrews 10:39)?

Dear Christian parents, please realize that the decisions you make for your children today will likely affect them for eternity. "Train up a child in the way he should go, even when he is old he will not depart from it" (Proverbs 22:6). Remember the words of Psalm 127:3-5:

> Behold, children are a gift of the LORD; the fruit of the womb is a reward. Like arrows in the hand of a warrior, so are the children of one's youth. How blessed is the man whose quiver is full of them; they shall not be ashamed, when they speak with their enemies in the gate.

God has placed the arrows in your hands. He has set up the targets and made it possible to reach them through Christ. Aim your children carefully. You only get one shot, so make it count for everything. Do all you can to help your children succeed. No sacrifice will be too great for you if it will help your children obtain that great inheritance.

Finally, I thank you for reading these letters and giving me your attention for awhile. I pray that God will bless you and your family as you live by faith and do His will. Although you and I may never meet in this world, I hope we may meet with our children and loved ones in the presence of God where there is fullness of joy and pleasures forever (Psalm 16:11). Until that glorious day, I leave you with these words from Jude 24-25 – "Now to Him who is able to keep you from stumbling, and to make you stand in the presence of His glory blameless with great joy, to the only God our Savior, through Jesus Christ our Lord, be glory, majesty, dominion and authority, before all time and now and forever. Amen."

Regards in the Lord,
Stacey

Glossary

Biblical Worldview – an understanding of all things that is founded upon the Bible

Common School – government school in which all children receive the same, universal education; the system of education founded in America by Horace Mann

Compulsory School – formal school in which attendance is compelled and forced by law

Convention of the Rights of the Child (CRC) – a treaty adopted by the United Nations as international law in 1989 which in effect takes away many parental rights and supplants them with government control

Darwinian Evolution – the theory advanced by Charles Darwin that declares all life to have evolved from lower forms of life by the natural process of mutations over eons of time

Education – the act of obtaining knowledge, skills, and abilities as well as morality and social skills

Establishment Clause – the following clause of the First Amendment of the U.S. Constitution: "Congress shall make no law respecting an establishment of religion"

Formal School – school that is taught by professional teachers in a classroom environment

Fundamental Right – a right that is virtually inviolable by government or any other party; a right that can be infringed by government only when it can prove a compelling interest under a high level of scrutiny in court

Government School – a term for compulsory school that emphasizes government control and funding

Homeschool – informal school that is administered to children by their parents

Humanism – a philosophy that embraces human reason and experience as the only guides for human life while rejecting Deity and revelation

National Education Association (NEA) – the main labor union that represents teachers and other educational professionals; the largest labor union and the largest professional organization in the United States

Patriotism – literally loyalty to one's fathers (from the Greek word *patrios*, which means "of one's fathers")

Positivism – a branch of humanism in which science is essentially substituted for God and the only truth is that which can be verified by science

Private School – formal school for a limited clientele that is administered by a non-government entity and is an alternative to compulsory school

Progressivism – a philosophy of gradual changes instituted by governmental intervention; rather than conserving what already exists, progressivism seeks for change; rather than causing change by sudden revolution, progressivism seeks to cause gradual change by evolution

Providence – God's foresight and gracious supplying of man's needs through natural means

Public School – formal school that is open to the general population

School – any institution in which instruction is given to children and young people

Secular – pertaining to worldly things that are not considered as religious or spiritual

Separation of Church and State – a rule of the U.S. Supreme Court for interpreting the Constitution taken from a phrase in a letter written by President Thomas Jefferson in 1802 to a Baptist association in Danbury, Connecticut

Social Darwinism – an evolutionary view of societies that corresponds to man's evolution of wisdom and technology

Socialization – the process of acquiring values, beliefs, and interactive skills found among the group of people in which one lives (society)

Sovereignty – the right and power to rule

Statism – a philosophy that considers the state (government) to be the ultimate authority in all things

Values clarification - a teaching method that imparts subjective morality to students and rejects objective standards

Index

www.ingramcontent.com/pod-product-compliance
Lightning Source LLC
Chambersburg PA
CBHW060921040426
42445CB00011B/727